Historic Manhattan Apartment Houses

ANDREW ALPERN

DOVER PUBLICATIONS, INC.
New York

Copyright

Copyright © 1996 by Andrew Alpern.
All rights reserved under Pan American and International Copyright Conventions.

Published in Canada by General Publishing Company, Ltd., 30 Lesmill Road, Don Mills,
Toronto, Ontario.
Published in the United Kingdom by Constable and Company, Ltd., 3 The Lanchesters,
162–164 Fulham Palace Road, London W6 9ER.

Bibliographical Note

Historic Manhattan Apartment Houses is a new work, first published by Dover
Publications, Inc., in 1996.

Library of Congress Cataloging-in-Publication Data

Alpern, Andrew.
    Historic Manhattan apartment houses / Andrew Alpern.
        p.   cm.
    Includes index.
    ISBN 0-486-28872-2 (pbk.)
    1. Apartment houses—New York (N.Y.)—History.   2. New York (N.Y.)—Buildings,
structures, etc.   3. Manhattan (New York, N.Y.)   I. Title.
    NA7862.N5A45   1995
    728'.314'097471—dc20
                                                                                        95-22141
                                                                                        CIP

Manufactured in the United States of America
Dover Publications, Inc., 31 East 2nd Street, Mineola, N.Y. 11501

Contents

Introduction v

Frontier French Flat 3
The innovative Imperial at 55 East 76th Street

Demonic Dorilton 6
Overblown ostentation at Broadway and West 71st Street

Broadway Bourgeois 10
Comforts at the Cornwall at 255 West 90th Street

Collapsed Capitol 13
Crashing concrete at 12 East 87th Street

Multi-Family Miscarriage 17
A housing experiment at 15 East 45th Street that failed

Venerable Verona 20
Mutilated mansion at 32 East 64th Street

Gainsborough Grandeur. 23
Soaring studios at 222 Central Park South

First on Fifth 25
Number 998 broke new ground

Hearst's Highrise 30
The ultimate tenant expansion at 137 Riverside Drive

Penthouse Pacesetter 33
Condé Nast's terraced duplex at 1040 Park Avenue

Appropriate Apartments 36
A battle for suitable scale at 655 Park Avenue

Soaring Salons 41
  Double-height grandeur at 1020 Fifth Avenue

Gracious Gracie 44
  A resplendent revolution on East 84th Street at the East River

Joyful Jacobethan. 51
  Musical inspiration at 1025 Park Avenue

Haute Hampshire 53
  From false starts to hotel to home at 150 Central Park South

Picturesque Pomander 60
  Apartments in a pseudo stage set on the Upper West Side

What Once Was on West End 64
  The grander days of 401 West End Avenue

Risky San Remo 67
  The best and worst of times on Central Park West

Neo-Luxury Normandy 72
  140 Riverside Drive marked the end of the Depression

Prewar Pioneer. 77
  Technological innovation at 25 East 83rd Street

Index 81

Introduction

The History of Manhattan's Apartment Houses Reflects the Diversity of the City's Peoples and Their Life-styles

OVER THE PAST century and a half, the range of living accommodations available in Manhattan has covered virtually every level of domestic architecture known in the United States. During the nineteenth century and again during the Great Depression of the thirties, those at the bottom of the social scale lived in squalid hovels thrown together with whatever materials were available for the taking. During the 1800s, these slums—no better than some of the worst parts of Bombay and Calcutta—were generally located in the undeveloped sections of the city, often among the rocky crags that had not yet been leveled to accommodate the newly mapped streets. But when the Great Depression hit, shack towns—called Hoovervilles after the unfortunate President who repeatedly promised that prosperity was just around the corner—sprang up wherever there was space, including the middle of the Great Lawn of Central Park.

Those a little more prosperous could live in tenement houses, the first of which may have been the one that appeared in 1833 on Water Street in the area now called the Lower East Side. Four stories high, it housed one family on each floor, making it a candidate for the city's earliest purpose-built multiple dwelling. In order to deal with the increasing flow of immigrants, more and more tenement houses were built for those who were referred to as "the laboring classes." By 1865, when the population of the city was approaching one million, there were 15,000 such buildings. They were pretty mean places in which to live and were the most visible sore on the skin of the city. As their inhabitants usually caused the most trouble for the authorities, periodic reform campaigns were mounted. Photographic muckrakers Lewis Hine and Jacob Riis helped to arouse more prosperous New Yorkers to alleviate the conditions of these poor people. Improvements were made, but tenement living was never more than the barest minimum of housing.

At the opposite end of the spectrum were the houses of those whose wealth could afford them almost unlimited choice. Until well into this century, their primary residences would only be individual houses, the most magnificent of these being little short of palaces. There was a surprisingly large number of such expansive edifices built in Manhattan during the period following the Civil War, when the country's aggressive economic expansion and the absence of an income tax provided ample opportunity for the massive accumulation of capital. Designed for lavish entertaining, these huge habitations required virtual armies of servants and enormous amounts of money to maintain. With the imposition of income taxes and the declining availability of domestic help after World War I, such ostentatious patterns of living became impractical and, by the mid-twenties, almost all of these mansions were gone. In their place rose apartment houses of all sorts, catering to a broad spectrum of economic and social levels.

Housing is a commodity like any other, and where there is a need, somewhere there is an ambitious entrepreneur who will fulfill that need. Particularly creative salesmen create needs where none exist by providing the solutions first and making them so desirable that people want them. To a large extent, that is how the apartment living styles of today evolved.

Prior to the Civil War, people who traveled extensively or who chose not to keep house lived in hotels. Those with very little to spend on housing lived in boardinghouses or in tenements. Anyone who was the least concerned with appearances—and that included just about everyone else—had to have his own roof over his head. That was true even if it were a rented roof and if that roof were not very far over his head—although the cost of it might well be. A person with even the least pretension to social standing would never consider maintaining his or her family in anything less than a private house. It could be a little frame dwelling, a sedate brownstone or a large and impressive mansion. But, modest or grand, it would house only one family; to share with strangers was unthinkable, and apartment houses were unheard of in New York.

But in the crowded cities of Europe, especially in Paris, apartment living was quite acceptable among the bourgeoisie. Thus, it comes as no surprise that a French-trained American architect designed what has often been credited as the first significant apartment house in Manhattan. Richard Morris Hunt built the Stuyvesant Apartments on East 18th Street in 1869–70 for Rutherford Stuyvesant. The building was commonly called The French Flats, and it offered a living style most New Yorkers were not quite prepared to accept. It was probably difficult for its first occupants to accept as well, since its planning was primitive, but it contained elements that clearly separated it from a tenement house and therefore made it suitable for middle-class rather than working-class tenants. Each apartment had a parlor for entertaining and a dining room for eating, with the kitchen relegated to a position as a service space, rather than being the central room of the house as would be the case in a tenement. There was indoor plumbing, not shared with another family, and there was even a small room for a servant. Clearly this was a home for a family that might consider itself at least moderately affluent.

As soon as it became evident that the new idea of French flats in Manhattan was not going to be totally disregarded by families seeking housing, builders and developers responded. A few such structures were raised in the 1870s, setting the stage for several ambitious projects that were built in the early 1880s. The Chelsea on West 23rd Street (built originally as housekeeping apartments) and the Central Park Apartments or Navarro Flats on West 59th Street, were designed by Hubert Pirrson & Company. The West 59th Street project was especially grand, with very large apartments, seemingly endless amenities and an underground vehicular tunnel leading from the street to provide unseen access for deliveries, a concept not to appear again on so large a scale until Rockefeller Center was built in the 1930s.

Nearby, the Osborne was designed by James E. Ware in the style of a massive Italian Renaissance palazzo, its interiors lavishly appointed in accordance with the latest fashions of decoration.

The most famous—the dowager Queen Mother of apartment houses—is, of course, the Dakota, at West 72nd Street and Central Park West. Built by Singer sewing machine heir Edward Clark to the designs of Henry Janeway Hardenbergh, its style is sometimes described as Brewery Gothic Eclectic, or, more waggishly, Middle European Post Office. The strategy Clark mounted to overcome the ever-present rental resistance included locating the building at one of the main entrances to the relatively new Central Park and a block away from a station of the Ninth Avenue elevated railway. He built substantial town houses in the vicinity to ensure a good neighborhood and—of course—he had Hardenbergh design the building in a very lavish manner. It originally contained an impressive array of service spaces, including a large wine cellar, extensive kitchens and a vast dining room for private parties—all of which have since been converted to additional apartments. The Dakota represented an elegant way of apartment living when it was first built, and it has retained that cachet to this day. It took four years of continuous work to complete the building, and the quality of its construction was designed to last for centuries. If the economics of the situation permit, perhaps it will.

These buildings were the most significant of the pioneers. But it was not until this century that the apartment house really began to develop. American architects were not very experienced in this area, and it often showed in the results. To compound the problem, profound differences were encountered in the projects. Certainly the design approach for a building to accommodate one 12-room apartment per floor on Park Avenue is quite different from that required for a building housing seven middle-class families per floor in upper Manhattan. As with any new product, consideration had to be given to the functional requirements as well as to the emotional needs and responses of the markets at which the new apartments were aimed. And there were basically two distinct markets for the apartments built up until the time of World War I. There were those families who had previously lived in brownstones or in other luxurious town houses but who wanted the convenience of an apartment dwelling. And then there were those who had lived in tenement buildings but whose standard of living had risen sufficiently to afford them a different style of living. Naturally, the type of accommodations, and where in the city they were to be provided, would be different for these two groups.

What we know as Manhattan's Upper West Side was one of the areas for apartment houses designed to cater to those who previously may have lived in some sort of private house. To counter the feeling that these new apartments were nothing more than glorified tenements, the builders made the gap between tenement and apartment living styles and amenities as wide as possible. The rooms were spacious, the apartments large, and touted in the advertising was the "high technology" of the day: central refrigeration and vacuum-cleaning systems, telephone switchboard services and triple-filtered tap water.

On the other side of the coin were the buildings constructed for the new middle class emerging from the tenements. In order to keep costs at a level that could be afforded by this market, the ventures were sited in the distant outreaches of Manhattan where the land was cheaper, but where in compensation there was more open light, air and expansive views.

A comparison of the floor plans of buildings typical of the two types of apartment development shows how different they were . . . and yet how similar the social conventions. The largest and grandest had a living room, a dining room, a kitchen, bedrooms and rooms for servants. But even minimal apartments in the outlying districts provided a formal dining room and often a servant's room, sometimes for a flat with only a single bedroom. Even if space was cramped, social custom dictated the inclusion of a dining room, and it usually served as the real "living" room of the house; the parlor was reserved for formal entertainment of visitors, a mark of respectability so important to those who were moving up in the world.

As the taste and demands of the apartment-consuming public became more sophisticated over time, and the builders became more skilled at their craft, apartment plans became more efficient. Rooms related better to their functions and to each other, space was more effectively distributed and apartments became more "livable."

What constitutes marketable livability in apartments, however, has altered with the changes in basic patterns of living, sometimes quite dramatically. Notwithstanding the existence of the Bauhaus in the 1920s, nothing but traditional furnishings and decorations would be acceptable to the wealthy householder of that period living in ten rooms on Fifth Avenue. Everything would be very elegant, in faultless good taste, but with the resultant ensemble likely to be stiff and conventional. Since World War II, an element of relaxed enjoyment of life has been introduced, with comfort and practicality figuring more strongly into the calculus than ritualistic formality. With a liberal variety of available choices, the living styles of affluent New Yorkers are dramatically different from those of 50 or 100 years ago. Where once a lavish bedroom had to emulate the grandeur of Versailles, today it is more likely to look like a cross between a computer center and a health-club gymnasium. Or it might be a chastely elegant minimalist composition of fine materials and stylized function. Reflecting those options, the architecture and interior detailing of expensive apartments are no longer elaborate or massive. Instead, rooms now present an anonymous and easily molded shell within which the imaginative designer can create a suitably individual environment for the occupant.

We bemoan the fact that "they don't build them the way they used to," but we conveniently forget about the societal restrictions and pressures that gave birth to those architectural imperatives. Ultimately, we recognize the economic realities of our world and the altered priorities we have developed. Where once we could accept a stratified society in which the undereducated, the disadvantaged and those with few personal resources merely toiled for the benefit of "their betters," we now require at least lip service to the concept of equal opportunity. Thus we can accept the concomitant changes in available living choices. The construction of ancient Rome depended on a slave-labor economy; the construction of the "grand old apartments" depended on cheap immigrant labor that worked beyond even the concept of fringe benefits. Today, labor-union demands and "entitlements" without responsibilities or effort dominate the budgets of municipalities and building developers alike. Just as we cannot turn back the clock on our concepts of how we ought to treat all human beings within our larger society, so too we cannot turn back the clock to the high-ceilinged and parquet-floored dwellings of long-dead days. But we can assuredly admire what was done in those past days and delve into the human stories behind the creation of what we now esteem.

Historic Manhattan Apartment Houses

Figure 1. A publicity rendering of the Imperial published in April 1883, a few months before the building opened. *(Courtesy of The New-York Historical Society.)*

Frontier French Flat

The Innovative Imperial at 55 East 76th Street

ONE OF THE earliest apartment houses still extant on the Upper East Side, the Imperial was completed in 1883 *(Figure 1)*. It is apparently exceeded in age only by the 1880 Manhattan at East 86th Street and Second Avenue, which has been under threat of demolition for some time, and it represents a pioneer outpost of multifamily construction in a neighborhood better known at the time for private houses and benevolent institutions *(Figure 2)*.

Although the first apartment house in New York was probably the Stuyvesant, which was completed on East 18th Street in 1870 *(Figure 3)*, it was not until a decade later that the concept of multiple dwellings for the middle classes (in contrast with tenements for the poor) began to gain enough of a foothold to warrant real-estate investments of any significant magnitude. A very modest five-family elevator apartment house was designed by Bruce Price at 21 East 21st Street in 1878, and the following year a comparable one (*sans* lift) was erected at 129 East 17th Street to plans drawn by Napoleon LeBrun. Both those buildings still exist, albeit in altered form.

The 31-unit Manhattan, in Yorkville, and the 39-unit three-building complex of 1881 known as the Windemere at West 57th Street and Ninth Avenue *(Figure 4)* were the earliest large projects to cater to those who worried about social requirements as much as spatial ones when seeking living quarters.

The suites these buildings provided, generally called French flats, included separate dining rooms and provisions for live-in domestic help—essential marks of bourgeois living. Developer Frederick Aldhous emulated these predecessors, but did so in a much more socially respectable area. Notwithstanding the smoke-belching locomotives running along Park Avenue half-a-block away, the East 76th Street site of the Imperial was sufficiently near the mansions of Fifth Avenue and the adjacent side streets to give it a location complementary to its middle-class apartments.

The building's design was by architect Frederick Theodore Camp, about whom little is known other than his lifespan (1849–1905), and the 1879 date of the establishment of his New York architectural practice with Gilbert Bostwick Croff. Camp's design, while primitive by later standards, showed an

Figure 2. The Manhattan of 1880, East 86th Street and Second Avenue, as it appeared in 1944. *(Courtesy of Christopher Gray.)*

understanding of what was essential to distinguish an apartment house from a tenement. There were three flats per floor, each with the requisite parlor and dining room, and with one or two servants' rooms. Dimensions were small, the largest living room being 12 feet by 18 feet, and each apartment had only one bathroom, but an attended elevator was provided and there were service dumbwaiters as well.

Developer Aldhous had strong feelings about fire safety, reflecting the concerns of his potential market. Horrendous tenement fires were a common occurrence during the nineteenth century, and fear of being trapped was a sales obstacle that had to be overcome before apartments could be rented. Aldhous addressed this issue by including three internal stairways in the Imperial. The external iron fire-escape stair may also have been an early installation to expand the perceptions of safety. Augmenting these measures was a standpipe system with a 7000-gallon roof tank and hoses at each floor, as well as electric alarms throughout the building and a night watchman to patrol the halls. These features, completely lacking in the tenements of the poorer classes, were given prominence in the press of the day, doubtless at the instigation of the owner.

Architecturally, the Imperial has a particularly distinctive façade. Constructed of brownstone, and detailed much like an oversized row house of the period, the building's Neo-Grec appearance is enlivened with carved enframements at each window, multiple belt courses with decorative iron railings and, at the top, a doubly pedimented cornice with corbels and denticulation. There had originally been an elaborate stone porch with polished granite columns protecting the entrance, but that was later removed and a simplified architrave installed instead. Apparently at that time the ground-floor decorative iron railings were installed. Because they match the ironwork on the fire escape, this work may all have been done at the same time. The grilles on the elevator cab are also similar and would date from the time when the lift's original hydraulic mechanism was replaced with an electric one. Thus, from aesthetic evidence alone (in the absence of any appropriate archival record), one can deduce a sequence of alterations and additions.

The Imperial was constructed at a reported cost of $90,000, which would not have included interior finishes or the price of the land. Rents in 1883 were listed at an average of $100 per month, and had not changed 30 years later, when they ranged from $75 to $116 per month. At that time the building was advertised as La Casa Blanca Apartments, the name change being a common ploy to increase rental interest in an older building.

The two- and three-bedroom apartments of the Imperial have been altered and rearranged over the years to reflect the changing needs of their occupants, but they have never been subdivided. The reason for this is probably because the building was bought by its tenants as a cooperative in 1920—one of the earliest conversions known.

The original architectural rendering of the building appears to be generally accurate, except for the possibly original fire escape that is not shown. The adjacent structures, however, are entirely fabrications. Appearing as neatly designed four-story flat blocks, these buildings were never built. In fact, the lots flanking 55 East 76th Street remained vacant for the first decade of the building's existence. Later, stables and carriage houses were built on both sides.

Below, left: Figure **3**. The Stuyvesant, 142 East 18th Street, may have been the first true apartment house in New York. It was razed in 1957; this photograph was taken in 1936. *(Charles von Urban, courtesy of the Museum of the City of New York.)*

Below, right: Figure **4**. The east façade of the Windemere in 1944, after the removal of the Ninth Avenue elevated railway. *(Municipal Archives, courtesy of Christopher Gray.)*

Demonic Dorilton

Overblown Ostentation at Broadway and West 71st Street

IF THE EAST SIDE was known for its elegant and refined apartment-house architecture, the West Side engendered an imagination gone wild among architectural designers at the turn of the century that reached its apogee (or its nadir, depending on your aesthetic sensibilities) in 1902 with the completion of the Dorilton, at 171 West 71st Street on the corner of Broadway *(Figure 5)*.

Brilliantly red brick mated with creamy white limestone and a tall black slate mansard roof yielded a color scheme that "yells 'Come and look at me,' " according to a critique published in *Architectural Record* shortly after the building was finished. Montgomery Schuyler, the acerbic magazine critic, went on to describe the effect of the structure on the passerby in language as colorful as the façade itself.

He complains that "everything shrieks to drown out everything else," and bemoans the "detestable spirit that reigns throughout" and that "sets the sensitive spectator's teeth on edge." He takes umbrage at the "stone balls on the gate posts of the entrance, two feet in diameter, left there for Titans to roll at ten pins," and criticizes the adjacent "cherubs carved with some blunt instrument that sprawl above the central gate" *(Figure 6)*. Finally, he pulls out all the stops and asserts that it is "an edifice which cannot be regarded with apathy, at the sight of which, on the contrary, strong men swear, and weak women shrink affrighted. As Carlyle says of the London statues: 'That all men should see this; innocent young creatures, still in arms, be taught to think this beautiful; and perhaps, women in an interesting situation look up to it as they pass? I put it to your religious feeling, to your principles as men and fathers of families!' "

The *New-York Daily Tribune* attempted to downplay the disparagement: "Whether the severe critic of architecture will approve its florid style matters little to the layman, who recognizes in the achievement a commendable effort toward a higher and more artistic form of architecture than is commonly attempted with buildings of this type."

But what of the Dorilton, which the New York City Landmarks Preservation Commission, in its 1974 designation report naming it an historic landmark, called "exceptionally handsome," and said it is "one of the finest Beaux-Arts buildings in Manhattan"?

Figure 5. The Dorilton in a view published in 1908 by G. C. Hesselgren in "Apartment Houses of the Metropolis." *(Collection of Andrew Alpern.)*

Figure 6. The exuberantly carved entry portal provoked outrage at the beginning of the twentieth century. *(Architectural Review, courtesy of Christopher Gray.)*

Planned in anticipation of the 1904 opening of the Broadway subway line, whose express station at West 72nd Street would make the building readily accessible to downtown, the Dorilton was the first of several large apartment houses to cluster around the new transportation nexus. Its developer was Hamilton M. Weed, about whom almost nothing is known. Only slightly more has been uncovered about its architects, Elisha Harris Janes and Richard Leopold Leo. Their firm, Janes & Leo, was formed in 1897 and apparently specialized in Beaux-Arts French Second-Empire brownstones and apartment houses, although they also produced a Neo-Gothic church in Harlem and a conventional Renaissance Revival tenement on West 80th Street near Riverside Drive.

The building Janes & Leo presented to Weed was a further development and inflation of the design concepts the firm had tried two years earlier with the Alimar, a much smaller apartment house at 925 West End Avenue. The form of the Dorilton follows the ideal of base/middle/capital, but in curiously high-waisted and low-shouldered proportions. It has a three-story rusticated limestone base, which has been crudely converted to stores at the ground floor along Broadway, but which is relatively intact on the side street, where it retains its original protective railing and moat.

The building's middle section is perhaps the most interesting now, as it is still close to its original conception. Particularly distinctive are the two Brobdingnagian, classically draped maidens serenely surveying the passing scene from their perch overlooking Broadway at the balustraded fourth floor *(Figure 7)*. Comparably unusual, along West 71st Street, are the two pairs of near-nude muscular men supporting (with great effort) iron-railed balconies at the sixth floor *(Figure 8)*.

Undoubtedly delightful (notwithstanding Montgomery Schuyler's ridicule of nearly a century ago) is the splendid entrance portal, which still recalls the halcyon days when the only filth in the streets came from horses.

Figure 7. Broadway belles? *(Andrew Alpern.)*

Figure 8. Weary atlantes midway up the façade of the Dorilton. *(Andrew Alpern.)*

The Dorilton was planned for middle-class families whose home life was sufficiently formal to require a dining room and accommodation for a live-in servant. These were provided for each of the four apartments per floor, which ranged from one- to four-bedroom units. There were large artists' studios at the top floor, an electricity-generating and refrigeration plant under the courtyard and storage rooms in the basement for each of the 48 apartments. Under the strictures of the rent-control laws, however, these flats did not generate enough profit to allow adequate maintenance of the building's ornamentation, and piece by piece much of it deteriorated and was removed.

It was only with conversion as a cooperative in 1984 that the depredations of decades began to be turned around. The tenant-owners have already begun the restoration process, and with patience, imagination and a large amount of money, the Dorilton may yet recover its lost outrageous glory.

Broadway Bourgeois
Comforts at the Cornwall at 255 West 90th Street

Most of the city's stock of solid and spacious West Side co-op apartments is in buildings that began as middle-class rental structures vying with each other to capture a fickle and demanding market. Those preceding World War I were especially vulnerable to changing tastes and shifting development patterns, as the custom of moving every year or two on October 1 was still prevalent. Architects and builders in the early years of the twentieth century strove to offer comfort, amenities and the accoutrements of the stolid bourgeois living style that was the goal of the "yuppies" of the time.

The Cornwall, at West 90th Street and Broadway *(Figure 9)*, was one of many such apartment houses on the Upper West Side constructed, according to the *New York Times* of July 24, 1910, as "the natural result of the city's increasing growth," and designed by the prolific architectural partnership of Thomas P. Neville and George A. Bagge. Formed in 1892 and dissolved about 1915, the firm was responsible for scores of West Side brownstones, small flat buildings and large apartment houses. Neville & Bagge enjoyed an increasingly successful practice; in 1909, the year that the Cornwall was begun, the firm filed plans for 57 buildings.

Upper Broadway in the nineteenth century had been expected to develop as a grand residential avenue (for a time it was actually called the Boulevard) and many blocks were still virgin land into the new century. On such a site Neville & Bagge designed an unusual 12-story apartment house for Arlington and Harvey Hall (representing the younger generation of a venerable New York development family). A massive block of limestone and brick, with an exuberance of carvings and decorative elements at the top three floors, the Cornwall is crowned with an openwork confection unique in New York. Curiously reminiscent of a particular small apartment house of 1902 in Vienna, this unusual alternative to the ubiquitous massive projecting cornice is one of the few gestures toward the Art Nouveau movement existing in Manhattan.

Inside, the architects originally provided three apartments to a floor—of seven, eight and nine rooms, with two or three bathrooms. Room sizes were not overly generous (living rooms were 13$\frac{1}{2}$ by 17 feet) but recessed sliding doors allowed an enfilade of living/dining/library to function en suite when more space for entertaining was needed. An innovative advantage of the lay-

Figure 9. The Cornwall, ca. 1944. *(Courtesy of Christopher Gray.)*

outs was the large entrance foyer for each unit, the "public" spaces of each apartment opening off them. Gone were the dreary long halls of only a few years earlier.

Similarly attractive to apartment renters were the "modern" six-burner gas stove in each kitchen, the combination gas-electric lighting fixtures, the wall safes in the bedrooms (equipped with combination locks and readily concealed with hanging pictures) and the central vacuum-cleaning system with hose connections in each apartment.

The rapid change in the perceptions of what was important to apartment living was evident in the filing of an alteration plan only four years after the building was completed. Corner apartments of eight rooms would get a second master bathroom at the sacrifice of one of the two maids' rooms. Changing tastes in buildings (or perhaps in neighborhoods) also yielded reduced rents: The most expensive apartment rented for $2800 (per *year*) in 1910, $2500 in 1914 and $2200 in 1916.

In grander neighborhoods, apartments were subdivided only when the Depression of the 1930s precluded expansive living for most New Yorkers, or when that was the only way to obtain market rents under the strictures of the "temporary" rent-control laws during World War II. At the Cornwall, however, apartments were cut in two as early as 1928, but most of the large units survived the years sufficiently intact to enjoy the benefits of a self-generated cooperative conversion in 1981, followed by a careful building restoration.

Limestone lavishness or gracious grandeur may be beyond the scope of many New Yorkers, but cooperative living can also be had as affordable affluence along Broadway.

Collapsed Capitol
Crashing Concrete at 12 East 87th Street

CONSTRUCTION MISHAPS ARE not common, and major building collapses are rare in New York. A particularly gruesome collapse occurred late in the afternoon on March 9, 1911. An eight-story apartment house was under construction on the south side of East 87th Street between Fifth and Madison Avenues, the superstructure already at the top floor and the concrete-and-block floor arches in place. Without warning, the arches of the top floor gave way and fell to the floor below. The concrete at that level collapsed under the sudden impact, and the lower floors failed in turn, like dominoes. The entire bay—top to bottom—went crashing into the cellar, taking four workers with it.

Under the headline "Accident to an Apartment House Intended for the Occupancy of Millionaires," the *Real Estate Record and Guide* reported the rumor that improperly placed concrete-mixer equipment on the top floor had precipitated the disaster, and noted that it had taken many hours of digging through the rubble to uncover the bodies of the dead workers. Faulty construction techniques had not been unusual with the cheaply built tenement houses of the nineteenth century, but such carelessness was rare at the site of a luxury apartment house such as 12 East 87th Street.

Originally called The Capitol, the building was designed by the innovative but largely unsung architectural partnership of George and Edward Blum. The brothers, both Paris-trained, had begun their practice in 1908 and specialized in apartment houses. Their work was highly original, and while it had overtones of the Art Nouveau style that was prevalent while they were studying at the École des Beaux-Arts, it also reflected the Arts and Crafts movement ascendant in the United States. The two brothers made extensive use of glazed terra-cotta, tile work and ornamental iron in distinctive forms of their own devising.

Following upon their first unusually decorative apartment building (the Phaeton, at 539 West 112th Street, 1909), the Blums designed six or eight more apartment houses of similarly inventive design. In 1910 they designed 12 East 87th Street with an entire front façade of terra-cotta masonry units and

Figure 10. 12 East 87th Street in 1911, when it had one apartment to a floor. Its appearance is little changed now despite subdivision of the apartments. *(Irving Underhill, courtesy of the Museum of the City of New York.)*

brick infilling worked into patterns that suggest carved stone *(Figure 10)*. Using ornamental detailing that cannot be placed into any particular historical period, they presented an apartment-house front unlike any other. The building's broad expanses of windows were unusual for the period, as was the deft handling of the decorative iron balconies that enliven the façade.

The apartments within this unique structure—one to a floor—were grandly spacious, yet exceptionally compact. Each had five bedrooms, three servants' rooms, a kitchen, a servants' hall and a separate, windowed laundry room. Of particular note were the four main reception rooms, each with a fireplace. These could open, one upon the other, to provide an entertaining space of 42 by 50 feet. The original rental notices suggested that adjacent apartments could be thrown together by means of a private staircase to provide grand duplex suites, and that the architects would be available to effect this or any other changes that tenants might require.

Following the reconstruction of the collapsed sections of the building, normal work on the building continued and the structure was completed in October 1911. Its large apartments rented well, as they enjoyed a well-developed neighborhood, and directly adjoined a large private garden. John S. Phipps had bought a full building lot, which he lavishly planted, next to his own five-story limestone town house. Rather than hiding his garden behind a high privacy wall, Phipps separated it from the street with only an ornamental iron fence and decorative gate for the enjoyment of passersby *(Figure 11)*. The apartments of The Capitol gained a benefit from this amenity as well, which helped to justify their high rents.

Figure 11. The garden of John S. Phipps, accessible from the Phipps residence to the west (right) and overlooked by the apartments of 12 East 87th Street (left). *(Collection of Andrew Alpern.)*

All went well for almost a quarter of a century but, as with so many large and expensive apartments during the Depression of the early 1930s, lease renewals became difficult to obtain. As an accommodation to the market's altered requirements, some of the apartments at 12 East 87th Street were subdivided in 1935. Then, in 1943, when the wartime rent-control laws placed ceilings on what could be charged for existing apartments, the remainder of the building was cut into smaller units for which market rents could be charged.

With four units to a floor instead of one, the building catered to a very different clientele from those who first lived there. And with the changed aesthetic sensibilities of the post-Depression era, the old Venetian Renaissance lobby decorations were no longer appropriate. Reflecting that "progress," a sleek new lobby of light wood tones, mirrors and zebra-striped upholstery was installed. A greater clash with the existing façade could hardly be imagined.

Nonetheless, the re-formed building remained fully rented over the years, and when it was converted to a co-op, its apartments joined the rarified precincts of haut-prix apartments a few steps from Central Park. Although 12 East 87th Street began life with a resounding crash, and weathered a different sort of crash 18 years later, its unusual terra-cotta front survives as a tribute to the inventive brothers who created it.

Multi-Family Miscarriage

A Housing Experiment at 15 East 45th Street That Failed

WHEN THE EIGHT-BUILDING Navarro apartment complex at Seventh Avenue and West 59th Street collapsed as a cooperative venture in 1883, the Home Club concept for communal living of Philip Hubert succumbed with it. It was only in the early years of the twentieth century that the idea of several families banding together to live in discrete apartments under a single roof regained a toehold in the New York residential market. Several specialized cooperative studio/apartment buildings, constructed by and for well-to-do artists in the early years of the century, have remained successful to this day.

One cooperative venture that failed rapidly was constructed in the heart of "club country" on East 45th Street, off Fifth Avenue. The neighborhood's socially secure position was established in 1893 with the construction of the Harvard Club at 27 West 44th Street, followed by the Century Club and the New York Academy of Medicine, both built on West 43rd Street in 1899.

In 1901, the Yale Club's 11-story clubhouse-cum-bachelor-apartments at 30 West 44th Street brought high-rise stability to the area. The strongly modeled structure was designed by Yale architecture-school graduates Evarts Tracy and Egerton Swartwout, who had recently set up their own practice following a stint with the eminent McKim, Mead & White.

Evidently flushed with their success with one sort of clubhouse, in 1906 Tracy and Swartwout joined forces with one Gordon to design a multiple dwelling dubbed the Home Club by its developer, banker Pliny Fisk. Aesthetically conceived as an overscaled Florentine palazzo, the building was constructed in limestone, brick and terra-cotta, with huge arched windows, a massive projecting cornice and a drive-in courtyard for carriages *(Figure 12)*.

On the second floor was a grand ballroom, 59 feet long, with a 25-foot-high ceiling and a palatial communal dining room 40 feet long. A full-time service and kitchen staff attended to the needs of the six families the building was designed to accommodate.

Each of the third through seventh floors was devoted to a 14- or 16-room apartment (with seven or eight baths apiece), while the top two floors comprised a duplex for Fisk and his family, including a solarium and play spaces on the roof for his children. For all this expansive grandeur, however, none of the apartments had kitchen facilities, as it was expected that all meals would

Figure 12. The Home Club in 1906. Grandiose semicommunal accommodations for six families. *(Wurts Brothers, courtesy of the Museum of the City of New York.)*

be taken in the second-floor banqueting hall. The cost of the building was said to be $300,000 (not including furnishings or decorations), and monthly maintenance charges were $1000 per unit (at a time when a genteel family could live for a year on less than half that sum). It is doubtful whether more expensive (or exclusive) apartments could have been had anywhere in the city at the time.

Pliny Fisk had been the prime mover behind the Ivy Club, Princeton's first eating club, and if he assumed that the camaraderie of his college days would survive the transition to large-scale family accommodations, he was wrong. Whether it was the rapidly changing neighborhood, or merely clashing personalities or life-styles among the resident owners, the cooperative was doomed as an apartment house.

In 1918 the building was expanded 25 feet to the east and converted to an apartment hotel by entrepreneur Charles Pierre, who ran a restaurant in the former private dining hall. A photograph of the time shows the entrance to the hotel at the base of the extension, with glass-fronted shops occupying what had originally been the ground-floor courtyard and reception spaces for the apartment house. Several years later, with the financial backing of others, Charles Pierre built the hotel at East 61st Street and Fifth Avenue that still bears his name. He was said to have been the last of the eponymous hoteliers, following the Delmonicos and Louis Sherry into history.

In 1921, after Pierre had made an interim move to 280 Park Avenue, the one-time Home Club's upper floors were converted to office space and the grand double-height entertaining spaces were altered to create additional normal-height offices as well. Cheap storefronts were built later on the ground floor to house a coffee shop and a cigar store, but from the fourth floor up, the façade is remarkably intact. If you look closely along this dingy side street, you can well imagine the splendor the quondam cooperative apartment house once held *(Figure 13)*.

Figure 13. The once-grand six-unit cooperative multiple dwelling, appearing in 1991 as a grade B side-street office building, hardly distinguishable from its neighbors. *(Gil Amiaga.)*

Venerable Verona

Mutilated Mansion at 32 East 64th Street

ONE OF THE finest of New York's early twentieth-century apartment houses was awarded a prize medal for its fine design by the American Institute of Architects, but then suffered the ignominy of having its wings clipped at the insistence of a quixotic neighbor. This vindictive virago triumphed over the well-placed owner of the Verona, and vandalized his masterful multiple dwelling by hacking off portions of its terra-cotta ornamentation.

Harriet A. R. Mills lived in a brownstone row house on Madison Avenue near the Baptist Church of the Epiphany, a large twin-towered Victorian Gothic church of 1882 that stood sedately at the southeast corner of East 64th Street and Madison Avenue. When the congregation sold its edifice to banker-turned-developer Col. Francis L. Leland, who razed it, along with the adjoining brownstone, Mrs. Mills found herself living next to a gaping 14-foot-deep excavation.

The new structure planned by Col. Leland, who was president of the New York County Bank, was to be a neo-Italianate palazzo loosely based on the design of the Strozzi palace in Florence. Instead of housing a single noble family, however, Leland's creation was to house 20, each in a grandly arranged 14-room apartment.

The architect was William E. Mowbray, whose family were builders and developers in Manhattan and Brooklyn during the late nineteenth and early twentieth centuries. Mowbray's façade design incorporated paired arched windows, belt courses and decorative balustrades and panels, set into a tan brick wall over a rusticated stone base, which in turn was protected behind a balustraded dry moat. Crowning this composition was a large and spectacularly intricate cantilevered cornice *(Figure 14)*. Curiously, this design, filed with the Department of Buildings in July 1907, was a virtual duplicate of the 1906 façade of the Home Club, at 15 East 45th Street designed by Gordon, Tracy and Swartwout *(see pages 17–19)*. Copyright protection for architectural designs did not then exist.

As originally planned, each apartment had a double entrance foyer, a spacious corner salon, an adjoining library and a large square dining room, as well as a billiard room (designated as an additional chamber on later plans). There were bedroom wings at opposite ends of the apartments, each with two chambers.

Figure 14. The Verona in 1922, before the insertion of shops into the Madison Avenue frontage, and with the adjoining brown-stone of Mrs. Mills still extant. *(Wurts Brothers, courtesy of the Museum of the City of New York.)*

The master suite, facing north onto East 64th Street, comprised two bedrooms with a huge connecting bathroom that boasted a grand recessed circular stall shower whose multiple levels of perforated annular piping could envelop the bather in a deluge of needle sprays.

The spaces within the apartments were planned with a careful attention to proportions and details. Each inner bedroom hall was subdivided by arches and moldings to reduce its apparent length, and had a semicircular niche at the end to provide a suitable spot for a piece of sculpture. Doors were thoughtfully placed to accommodate furniture arrangements, and five fireplaces were provided in each apartment.

Original tenants who signed leases prior to the completion of construction were given the option of specifying changes from the standard plans. As a result, several of the floors were modified to provide three apartments instead of two, although the resulting suites are still grand by any standards. One of them, a nine-room unit, was advertised in 1990 for $3.7 million (original rents in the building ranged from $5500 to $11,500 annually).

Part of the attraction of the building was (and remains) the grand entrance, with bronze torchères flanking the arched entry, and a finely crafted double marble staircase with an intricate decorative iron railing in the lobby. The exterior steps bridge the moat, which is still extant on the side street, although it was removed along the avenue when shopfronts were installed there in 1926.

All this was of no import to Harriet Mills, however, who doubtless resented the intrusion of an overbearing tenement into her formerly low-scale neighborhood. Several months after construction had begun, Mrs. Mills and Victor Kranich, president of Col. Leland's development company, signed a document in which the builder was permitted to extend the Verona's cornice and ornamental terra-cotta decorations several feet along the structure's southern wall, thereby overhanging Mrs. Mills's brownstone and intruding minimally into her unoccupied air space. In return, Kranich agreed for Col. Leland to reconstruct the stoop and railing of the Mills brownstone to the owner's satisfaction and to accommodate the encroaching north wall of the brownstone within the south wall of the new apartment house.

Mrs. Mills must have been a masterful negotiator, for there was a further stipulation that no permanent easement was being granted, and that, upon 90 days' notice from Mrs. Mills or "her legal representatives or assigns," the builder was forthwith to remove the overhanging cornice and moldings at his own cost. A final twist of the knife gave Mrs. Mills the right to remove the offending stonework herself if it were not lopped off fast enough upon her order, and a $3000 bond was to be provided to ensure that the woman's instructions would be followed.

Less than four years later, Mrs. Mills decided to exercise her option, and ordered Col. Leland to lobotomize his building. When he refused, she won a court order authorizing her to do the work herself. She then hired some laborers who smashed off the delicate ornamentation, leaving the broken internal structure of the terra-cotta exposed to the elements. For many years this depredation could be seen from Madison Avenue, but during a recent restoration of the façade, the scars were smoothed over with stucco. As for Mrs. Mills, she died not long after her act of mutilation, her obituary noting her eccentric ways.

Gainsborough Grandeur
Soaring Studios at 222 Central Park South

NOW HEMMED IN by bland modern apartment houses of no distinction, the Gainsborough Studios originally stood out visually and functionally as a building conceived and constructed to meet a very specialized need as living/ working spaces for successful artists *(Figure 15)*.

Figure 15. The Gainsborough Studios when it was dramatically different from its neighbors; today only the details of its façade distinguish it from the adjoining buildings. *(Wurts Brothers, courtesy of the Museum of the City of New York.)*

A common complaint of artists who enjoyed social and financial success at the beginning of the twentieth century was the dearth of suitable north-light studio space that would also be appropriate for showing their work to their similarly well-heeled and socially conscious clients. A group of such artists, led by Henry Ranger and Walter Russell, had solved the problem by organizing a corporation and constructing for themselves a cooperative studio/apartment house at 27 West 67th Street. Completed in 1903, the building incorporated double-height studios, along with conventional living spaces, and was so well received that two more were completed on the block by 1907.

Taking the cue from the West 67th Street enclave, another group of like-minded artists acquired a 50-foot site on Central Park South in 1907 and completed a comparable building the following year.

Unlike the speculator-built "bankers' studios" for those who merely wanted extra-large entertaining spaces, the Gainsborough was intended as working spaces for real artists. Thus, the double-height studios overlooked Central Park (more for the diffuse north sky than for inspirational views), huge windows being provided to capture as much of the daylight as possible. Planned and financed by three working artists and a businessman, the Gainsborough was designed to accommodate the private needs of its artist-owners, and to serve as a public advertisement of its artistic function.

August Franzen was a portrait painter whose work now hangs in the National Gallery of Art and the Brooklyn Museum. As president of the building's cooperative corporation, Franzen was undoubtedly responsible for the structure's name, as he had admired and emulated the work of the eighteenth-century painter Thomas Gainsborough.

Emphasizing the artistic connection is a portrait bust of Gainsborough within a shrine-like enclosure at the second floor, and an allegorical sculptural frieze across the entire façade at that level, both executed by the then-well-known sculptor Isidore Konti. Complementing these elements is a facing of multicolored Moravian tiles at the top two floors of the building, along with a scalloped crown molding to replace the usual projecting cornice that would have cast a shadow onto the top-floor windows.

The architect who integrated this façade with the building's distinctive duplex-studio arrangement was Charles W. Buckham, who also designed several other studio buildings for artists and those who sought an artistic ambience. The interior grandeur of Buckham's apartments at the Gainsborough attracted owner-residents who altered and expanded the original layouts, in some cases creating huge studios spanning the entire width of the building.

In the late 1950s, the residents retained designer Donald Deskey (of Radio City Music Hall fame) to redesign their lobby and to alter the entrance. The original wrought-iron doors and classical detailing gave way to the inappropriate modernity of glass and steel. A quarter century later, however, the tide had turned, and an historically accurate restoration was undertaken. Prompted by severe deterioration of the façade stonework, a complete re-creation of the Konti frieze and bust was done, along with a total replacement of the upper-level decorative tiles, a restoration of the lobby and a reconstruction of the wrought-iron doors to match photographs of those Deskey had trashed.

At a cost of over a million dollars, the restoration project was self-driven by the members of the cooperative. The mandatory oversight of the Landmarks Preservation Commission came only when the building was designated in 1988, well after the work had been begun.

Missing only its original decorative iron balconies at each floor, the Gainsborough Studios now closely replicates its 1908 appearance, and still provides grand accommodations for artists (several still use the building for studio space) and for those connected with the arts as creators or appreciators.

First on Fifth

Number 998 Broke New Ground

NINE-NINETY-EIGHT FIFTH AVENUE was a potentially troubled building from the start. First, it was to be erected on one of the few neighborhood sites that was not encumbered by height restrictions (anything tall was sure to raise howls from local mansion dwellers). Second, multifamily buildings were still not acceptable to the established upper classes—the market the builders hoped to attract. Apartments had been available in New York for 40 years, and there had even been an earlier one on Upper Fifth—a six-story middle-class structure appropriately called the Fifth Avenue Apartment House, completed in 1890 on the southeast corner of East 85th Street. The grander apartment houses such as the Dakota (1884) and the Osborne (1885) were financially successful, but for the truly wealthy and socially conscious, private row houses with high ceilings and expansive rooms remained de rigueur.

Developers Charles R. Fleischmann and James T. Lee recognized the obstacles and planned a structure that would please apartment-seekers and smooth the feathers of neighborhood reactionaries. Their scheme worked. The apartment house, designed by the architectural firm of McKim, Mead & White in 1910, was completed in 1912 *(Figure 16)*. (The building, however, lacked any contribution from Stanford White, who had been shot to death four years earlier by jealousy-crazed madman-playboy Harry K. Thaw.) The building's accommodations rivaled all but the most palatial private houses, the contemporary press lauding it as possessing "quiet dignity and an air of substantiality" and being "the most remarkable thing of its kind in America" *(Figure 17)*.

The building *is* superb inside and out. Its 12-story limestone façade, subdivided horizontally into three sections, is crowned with a massive stone cornice surmounted by a gently pitched, copper-clad roof. The stone blocks of the base section are rusticated, with carved stone escutcheons separating the windows at the fourth floor. A balustraded belt course defines the start of the middle section, the windows at that level having strongly modeled pediments. Intricately articulated corner quoins add visual strength to the middle and upper sections and create a finely wrought counterpoint against the smooth planar limestone upper walls. A broad planting strip along the avenue and a lesser one on the side street create a vestigial "moat." The entrance on East 81st Street

Figure 16. 998 Fifth Avenue under construction, as seen from within Central Park, April 26, 1911. *(Courtesy of the Museum of the City of New York.)*

is protected by an unusually wide marquee (an elegant alternative to the ubiquitous canvas awning), which was once fully glazed and splendidly ornamented *(Figure 18)*. Iron-and-glass canopies were once popular in fine New York apartment houses, but most were lost from lack of careful maintenance. This marquee survives, but in a considerably diminished state.

Figure 17. A building of "quiet dignity and an air of substantiality." *(Irving Underhill, courtesy of the Museum of the City of New York.)*

Figure 18. The marquee at the entrance to 998 Fifth Avenue, as originally fully glazed and ornamented. *(Collection of Andrew Alpern.)*

Inside, the architects and consulting engineers fitted out the apartment house with considerably more care and substance than might have been expected in what was essentially a speculative venture. The building had an extra-capacity heating system and fully concealed steam radiators, as well as central refrigeration and ice-making plants. Although mains were connected to New York Edison Company lines, the basement also had space for steam-driven electrical generators, should they be needed. A mechanical ventilation system removed kitchen cooking odors and guarded against down drafts in the building's two garbage-incineration systems. There were also a central vacuum-cleaning system, jewelry and silver safes anchored in the walls of each apartment, remote laundries with ventilated steam-drying devices, basement storage rooms, refrigerated wine cellars and additional servants' quarters on the roof.

Figure 19. The standard stair design for the duplex apartments at 998 Fifth Avenue, this one seen ca. 1919 in the suite of Ludwig Dreyfous. (Architectural Review, *collection of Andrew Alpern.*)

To further entice mansion-dwellers to relocate to the new structure, the rental brochure (a hardcover book with engraved illustrations) stressed that rooms' sizes and servants' quarters and facilities were better than those in any but "the most pretentious of private houses." The publicity also highlighted the conveniences of apartment houses: The chores of tending to complex building needs were left to others; a unit could be closed with ease during a family's absence, the superintendent taking charge at a moment's notice, seeing to interim cleaning and ventilating, and preparing for the occupant's return. "In these days of frequent trips abroad or to country estates," said the brochure, "the advantages of the multiple dwelling will doubtless appeal to many people."

Only 17 suites were originally planned for the building, with annual rents ranging from $10,000 to $26,000 for 14 to 17 rooms. Facing Fifth Avenue was a large simplex with a 36-foot-long wood-paneled reception hall leading to a circular or octagonal small salon separating the living room from the dining room, each with a working fireplace. At the east side of the building, on the side street, stacked duplex suites were planned (*Figure 19*). Special apartments were arranged by combining some of the units before they were occupied. One of the largest, 22 rooms and 8 bathrooms, taking up the entire tenth floor and a portion of the eleventh, was rented by former Senator Elihu Root. Root had formerly lived in a large house at East 71st Street and Park Avenue that had been designed for him in 1903 by architects Carrère & Hastings. He surprised the public by selling it and moving into 998 Fifth.

Although it was widely reported that Root would pay the incredible annual rental of $25,000 for his new apartment, Douglas Elliman, then a fledgling salesman in his older brother's real-estate firm of Pease & Elliman, revealed in 1964 that he had used the senator as a "loss leader" to fill the building. Rather than the announced price, Root was given the "bargain" rate of $15,000 in the hope that he would draw others of similar status. The ruse worked, and apartments were taken by Murray Guggenheim, Mrs. Elliott Finley Shepard (granddaughter of Commodore Cornelius Vanderbilt) and Levi P. Morton, formerly a New York State governor and Vice President of the United States.

A few years after it opened, 998 was sold at a significant profit, and it changed hands several times at ever-increasing prices until it was converted to a cooperative in 1953. When sold, each apartment generally now commands several times what the entire building originally cost. Advertised prices over the past few years have included $5.1 million for a 13-room duplex maisonette with a conservatory and an 1800-square-foot garden, $5.5 million for a 15-room suite with 11-foot ceilings, and $8 million for a full-floor 9000-square-foot flat.

According to the building's 1974 Landmarks Preservation Commission designation report, it is "the finest Italian Renaissance-style apartment house in New York City." The only regret is that more like it were not erected.

nection points within each apartment. According to the assertions of a contemporary rental advertisement, tenants could enjoy "every modern improvement that modern building science has been able to produce." The building was completed in time for the fall renting season of 1907, and despite the financial panic of that year, annual rents for the flats were pegged at a hefty $3000 to $4500.

Hearst arranged with McDonald for a lease of the top three floors and a penthouse roof garden, with the plans altered to give him a suitable layout for housing his large-scale collections and his even-larger-scale entertaining.

The arrangement worked well for several years, but with the continuing growth of both his family and his assemblage of things, Hearst needed more space. In 1913 he sought to persuade his landlord to allow him to expand his triplex down to the eighth and ninth floors and to make dramatic alterations to the resulting five-floor suite. When McDonald was understandably reluctant to subject his building to such drastic surgery, Hearst offered to buy the entire building instead.

To meet the reported $950,000 price, Hearst took a mortgage loan for $525,000 from the Mutual Life Insurance Company. He then began a remodeling program that took a decade to complete and resulted in a suite of grand multistoried rooms that one might more reasonably associate with San Simeon, his vast castle in California, than with a mere apartment in a multiple dwelling shared with other families. The renovation included replacing a large portion of the building's roof with a giant raised skylight room to illuminate the rooms below, and destroying all traces of the original two-apartments-per-floor room configurations.

The two-storied living room he created was a cavernous affair with heavily carved woodwork, a huge stained-glass window and recessed cabinets to house a collection of oversized silver salvers. There was a Georgian dining room, a French Empire bedroom and bits and pieces of almost every other architectural and decorating style that ever existed. Perhaps the most archetypal "Hearstian" room, however, was the triple-height vaulted stone hall that housed a ghost army of armored retainers *(Figure 20)*.

Hearst expanded this grand living style during the 1920s, but then contracted it under financial pressures in the thirties. The ultimate insult came in 1938, when the Mutual Life Insurance Company foreclosed on its mortgage and wrested the building's ownership away from the one-time tycoon.

The company then gutted the building and structurally filled in the missing floors of the extra-height rooms. It reconstructed the Clarendon and spent $300,000 of prewar money to provide 60 small apartments—five to a floor—of three to five rooms each. New internal fire stairs were constructed, the elevators upgraded, the lobby redesigned, and the rooftop skylight room became a penthouse studio. The completed apartments were rented out, but as with so many other West Side buildings, what was eventually uneconomical for the landlord under the strictures of the rent-control laws became a working proposition for multiple owners under a cooperative scheme. As a co-op, the Clarendon has been restored—not to its original lavish state, but rather as a hybrid that recalls the original 1907 luxury of its metal-and-glass marquee, as well as the changes in the apartment configurations that were wrought in 1939.

Penthouse Pacesetter
Condé Nast's Terraced Duplex at 1040 Park Avenue

ALTHOUGH HE WAS not the first to utilize a rooftop for an expanded residence, the publisher Condé Nast was the earliest exponent of terrace entertaining, and perfected the art of sumptuous and well-planned penthouse parties. His aerie at 1040 Park Avenue, with its attached greenhouse, established the penthouse apartment as the pinnacle of prosperous living *(Figure 21)*.

Figure 21. 1040 Park Avenue in 1925, the terraced upper level of Condé Nast's duplex penthouse just visible above the iron-balconied top floor of the building. *(Wurts Brothers, courtesy of the Museum of the City of New York.)*

33

Figure 22. The northwest corner of Park Avenue and East 86th Street, site of 1040 Park Avenue, in 1921. *(Courtesy of The New-York Historical Society.)*

Prior to the mid-1920s, apartment-house roofs were given over to elevator machinery and water tanks. Occasionally they were also used for accommodating janitors' apartments or additional maids' quarters, but rooftop living for socially self-conscious New Yorkers was almost unheard-of. The concept of terraced country living in the city had yet to emerge.

At least one early attempt had been made to use an apartment-house roof more creatively, however. Architect Julian Clarence Levi was living in 1905 in an apartment on the top floor of a since-demolished building at West 81st Street and West End Avenue. At the time, there was nothing blocking the view of the Hudson River from the upper floors. However, the Levis' apartment faced an inner courtyard.

Levi approached the building's owner and proposed that he be allowed to cut through the roof and install a circular stairway that would connect his apartment to an enclosed gazebo and open-air deck that he would construct on the roof. Although his landlord was sympathetic, and was convinced that Levi would erect a well-constructed and tastefully designed adjunct to his apartment, he declined to grant permission. His response was, "Mr. Levi, when you move out at the end of your lease, what will I do with your stairway and your gazebo? Who would ever want to live on a roof!"

Architects Delano & Aldrich had similar thoughts when they designed 1040 Park Avenue for the J. H. Taylor Construction Company to replace a welter of tiny nineteenth-century wooden cottages *(Figure 22)*. The plans they filed with the Department of Buildings in 1923 called for three spacious apartments of eight, 11 and 12 rooms, on each floor. On the roof, they showed servants' quarters for rental to those lower-floor tenants who required more than the two or three maids' rooms their apartments provided.

In 1924, before those upper spaces could be constructed, revised plans were filed to create a grand duplex penthouse for Condé Nast. The gregarious and successful publisher of *Vogue* and *Vanity Fair* had been living at 470 Park Avenue, which provided him with a conventional four-bedroom apartment.

While spacious for a man whose divorced wife no longer lived with him and whose children had grown up and left, it was insufficient to accommodate his entertaining style, which was at least as much business-related as it was social.

The new digs Nast planned encompassed the rooftop space, plus one of the top-floor apartments. The standard corner apartment was reduced by giving one of its rooms to the adjoining suite. It was then reworked to provide six bedrooms plus a small room and bath for Nast's valet. A simple two-run straight stair was constructed to connect these rooms with the "public" floor above. There, in addition to further servants' quarters, a kitchen and a dining room, were the three primary entertaining spaces: a library, a 28-foot drawing room and the centerpiece, a 43-foot salon, which served as a ballroom.

After redecorating the little house she shared with Elisabeth Marbury on East 17th Street and impressing architect Stanford White in 1898 with its freshness and elegant simplicity, Elsie de Wolfe gave up her acting career and became America's first professional interior decorator. The social *beau monde* quickly noticed her and liked the way she made rooms bright and cheerful. By the 1920s, de Wolfe was subjecting large numbers of expensive apartments to the French look she admired.

Nast joined her list of clients and received an especially lavish hand. Filling the rooms with pale green damask, mauve-gray silk and delicate Savonnerie carpets, de Wolfe assembled large quantities of antique and reproduction French furniture, setting the pieces off with trompe-l'oeil wall treatments of grisaille moldings, marbleizing and imitation wood paneling. The total effect that she produced was designed to look its best at night, and sparkled in a way that created a shimmering backdrop for the festivities that were anticipated.

Nast inaugurated his new home with a dinner party and dance in January 1925. It was a glittering affair that included the Alfred Lunts, the Efrem Zimbalists and the Arthur Hammersteins, as well as Katharine Cornell, Jascha Heifetz, George Gershwin, Frank Crowninshield, Edward Steichen, Fred Astaire and Edna St. Vincent Millay. As with all his future entertainments at the 1040 penthouse, Nast's staff recorded the attendance figures, measuring them against the weather conditions and the number of days in advance that the invitations went out. Records were kept of what was eaten, what liquors were consumed and even what furniture was used, in addition to who served as staff for the event. Cost records were also kept, perhaps more for tax reasons than anything else.

A year later, Delano & Aldrich extended the functional space of the apartment by installing a glazed conservatory along most of the south terrace, thus permitting even larger fêtes to be mounted.

This lavish penthouse served Condé Nast well until his death in 1942 at the age of 68. Not long after, his apartment was subdivided into five separate units. The large lower floor apartments also proved financially unwieldy under the combined strain of the Depression and the rent-control laws, and they too were cut into smaller units. Ultimately the building gained a new lease on life through conversion to cooperative status, and it is in this state that it exists today.

Appropriate Apartments
A Battle for Suitable Scale at 655 Park Avenue

SIX-FIFTY-FIVE PARK AVENUE is strikingly different from the other grand apartment houses that line most of that exclusive residential avenue. Less lofty than the others, it also is bifurcated with an elegantly fenced square of greenery that opens onto a peaceful interior landscaped courtyard *(Figure 23)*.

The relatively smaller-scaled domestic ambience of number 655 was the compromise consequence of an early effort toward "contextual" design—something that would be a suitable neighbor for the surrounding town houses. It exists because some very wealthy and influential nearby residents were afraid of what might be built to replace the former hospital on the site. So difficult was the accomplishment, however, that a first attempt in 1922 failed to produce a financially viable project, and it was only in 1924 that a new investment group was able to achieve the result that now exists.

The grand apartment houses of Fifth Avenue and Park Avenue are treasured as historic landmarks and are protected from destruction or inappropriate change by the strictures of New York City's strong Landmarks Law. In 1919, however, many Upper East Siders looked upon the proliferating multiple dwellings merely as casters of long shadows and intruders upon an otherwise gracious neighborhood of private residences. So great was the perceived threat, in fact, that a group of the area's property owners banded together to prevent the development site at Park Avenue and East 68th Street from being "improved" with yet another bourgeois behemoth of a towering tenement.

The impetus for this circling of the gilded wagons was Hahnemann Hospital's need for more space. The hospital was one of a group of civic institutions that had been constructed on land originally set aside by the city as the site for a public park called Hamilton Square. Part of the Commissioners' Map of 1811 (the first—and some say the only—piece of city planning New York accomplished), the park covered the area from East 66th to 68th Streets, and from Fifth to Third Avenues. It was opened in 1817, but the completion of Central Park made the diminutive city-owned pleasure ground superfluous, and in 1869 it was decommissioned, the streets cut through and the lots apportioned for more practical public purposes.

Figure 23. 655 Park Avenue in the summer of 1924 as its interior was being finished. *(Joseph Smith, courtesy of The New-York Historical Society.)*

Among the institutional buildings erected on the former park land were a police station, the headquarters of the fire department, the Institute for Deaf Mutes, the Baptist Home, the Seventh Regiment Armory and Hahnemann Hospital.

The hospital had been in the forefront of the homeopathic medical movement of the nineteenth century and had prospered, along with the nearby Presbyterian Hospital at East 70th Street and Lenox Hill Hospital (originally the German Hospital) at East 77th Street and Park Avenue. By 1917, Hahnemann had successfully petitioned the City for title to the land under its building, a 125-foot-deep property that encompassed the entire easterly blockfront on Park Avenue from East 66th to 67th Streets. Needing larger quarters, it acquired an essentially vacant 30,000-square-foot site at East 106th Street and Fifth Avenue. In 1919, it simultaneously began construction of a new building, and put its Park Avenue property up for sale.

In reaction to this move, under the aegis of Douglas Elliman a syndicate was formed by owners of nearby mansions. Percy Pyne, William Sloane, George Blumenthal, Arthur Curtis James, Harold Pratt and several others purchased the hospital site in joint venture and attempted to find similarly prosperous people who might be willing to construct private houses on the site.

It quickly became evident that the potential for new mansions in the neighborhood was minimal, so the syndicate devised a scheme that would provide apartment accommodations while still preserving the ambience of the members' private-house enclave. The never-to-be-built results of the planning were announced on March 26, 1922, four months before the hospital was scheduled to move to its new quarters (with a simultaneous name-change to Fifth Avenue Hospital).

The socially well-placed architectural firm of Delano & Aldrich had been hired to design a building that would retain the scale and character of a private house, and that would provide house-like apartments of grand proportions. Perhaps still thinking in terms of pre–World War I tastes and needs, the architects clearly missed the mark.

Delano & Aldrich had prepared the plans for the Knickerbocker and Colony Clubs, and were well experienced at designing private houses in New York. The building they devised for the hospital site was actually three separate structures grouped around a central entrance courtyard facing Park Avenue (arcaded on three sides and protected by a manned gatehouse). Each of the three buildings had four quadruplex maisonette apartments (all with private elevators), stacked two upon two.

Off the courtyard arcade, each of these residences had a private entrance that opened onto a spacious reception room. For the lower units, this level also housed the kitchens and other service spaces. (These functions were housed on the top floor for the upper units.) Each apartment had a floor of "entertaining" rooms comprising a very large drawing room and a dining room whose dimensions were not much smaller. Ceiling heights at this level were to be 15 feet in the clear. Two bedroom floors accommodated a total of six master bedrooms plus an equal number of servants' rooms, and all rooms faced the street, the entrance courtyard or one of the two formally planted gardens. As projected in the publicity for the venture, each unit was to have "the advantages of an apartment while retaining the more exclusive character of a private house." A newspaper article of the time said that the architects' brief was to produce "house apartments rather than an apartment house."

In designing this residential complex, the architects were clearly emulating the similar 1885 project of McKim, Mead & White for Henry Villard at Madison Avenue and East 50th Street, in which six private houses were clustered around an entrance courtyard in a way that gave the impression of a single grand mansion of palatial proportions. Railroad magnate Henry Villard masterminded that cooperative venture, but each unit was owned outright by its resident family. In the case of the Delano & Aldrich project, however, the "house apartments" were to be split evenly between cooperative tenant-ownership and ordinary rental status. Occupancy was projected for autumn 1923.

By January of that year, however, it was obvious that even this compromise mansion/apartment plan was not viable, and the neighborhood syndicate sold the then-vacant property to Dwight P. Robinson & Company for multifamily cooperative occupancy. Nonetheless, the protective sellers retained the last word by imposing a height restriction that effectively barred the construction of yet another of the 15-story apartment houses that they considered so objectionable.

Robinson hired architects James E. R. Carpenter and Mott B. Schmidt, who designed the uniquely low-scaled multiple dwelling with side-street entrances and a garden courtyard that was actually built. It was given the address of 655 Park Avenue. Rising to only eight stories at the East 67th Street end of the westerly avenue elevation, the structure is three stories taller along its eastern side. The uphill rise going north along Park Avenue removes the lowermost story at East 68th Street, giving the building an even more modest appearance at that point.

Presenting an English Georgian front to complement the still-extant block of mansions on the west side of Park Avenue between East 68th and 69th Streets, the red and white brick-and-limestone façade of the Carpenter/Schmidt building includes eight-over-eight multipaned windows characteristic of the Georgian architectural style, as well as appropriately designed stone window heads, corner quoins and parapet balustrades.

The floor plans developed by the architects comprised simplex apartments of eight to 11 rooms, plus one duplex of 14 rooms. Besides the terraced penthouse units, there are two eighth-floor apartments at the setback level. Each of these enjoys a 2800-square-foot terrace with three exposures and frontage directly on Park Avenue.

According to the *New York Times*, William K. Vanderbilt, Jr., bought a duplex maisonette apartment with its own street entrance, signing the contract in December 1923, almost a year before the building's construction was completed. (Two years later, his wife bought her own large maisonette apartment across the avenue at number 660.) In October 1924, the *Times* reported that the apartment-ownership rolls of 655 Park Avenue also included the architect and indefatigable chronicler of Manhattan iconography Isaac Newton Phelps Stokes, former minister to China Charles R. Crane and Bank of America vice-president E. A. De Lima. Each purchased his apartment under a lease of 99 years, with the purchase prices ranging from $20,000 to $66,000. Today, those figures would be barely enough to buy a small fraction of one room in the building!

In 1919, the group to which Hahnemann Hospital sold its property vainly sought buyers for six or eight private houses on the Park Avenue property. In 1922, the same group was unsuccessful in marketing 12 maisonette apartments designed for the site. Finally, in 1924, 655 Park Avenue was completed—an unusually low apartment building, yet one housing 51 families. The structure represents the last gasp in an ill-fated attempt to maintain a low-scaled, low-density domestic neighborhood in a part of Manhattan that arguably can be considered the most coveted residential area in the entire country.

The Pratt/Pyne/James consortium of 1919 sought to freeze-frame their portion of New York and block its natural development. The city had been growing ever taller and more dense in a relentless progression since its first colonization in 1624, and was not about to stop merely because a group of rich and influential people wanted it to do so. In the early 1800s, reactionaries complained that the five-story commercial buildings were overbearingly large when compared with the existing structures of the 1700s. Later in the century, when Elisha Graves Otis' newly invented elevator was made safe and practical, the resultant 10-story "towers" were said to be plunging the city into perpetual shadow. It was asserted that they created intolerable overcrowding of the streets and they overtaxed the city's resources and services. For the Pratt/Pyne group, a 15-story apartment house translated to "overdevelopment," and was to be opposed in much the same way earlier "tall" buildings were fought.

By the 1930s, 30-story skyscrapers were preached against as immoral. They were said to represent the evils that spawned the biblical Tower of Babel, and critics sought to prevent their construction. Today, overzealous "preservationists" often attempt to block any development project that is taller than its neighboring buildings.

If the ultraconservatives who fight to maintain the *status quo* in every generation had been allowed to have their way from the start, New York would still be a little village of three-storied houses. If the reactionaries had prevailed in the late nineteenth century, we would not possess much of the architecture now designated as landmarks. And if the zealots of today impose their will on the city (quoting the Prince of Wales much as the critics of the nineteenth century quoted scripture), the greatest city in the world will gradually atrophy and die.

New York must constantly rebuild itself so that its physical plant can keep pace with the intellectual development of its citizens and the economic progress of its commercial enterprises. But where are the architects who can design buildings that have the elegance and grace of its finest apartment houses— buildings like 655 Park Avenue?

Soaring Salons

Double-height Grandeur at 1020 Fifth Avenue

APARTMENTS WITH EXTRA-HEIGHT ceilings are a rarity in New York, but there are six such units at 1020 Fifth Avenue, one duplexed to a terraced penthouse. The architectural firm that provided these lavish units was the partnership of Whitney Warren & Charles Delevan Wetmore, better known as the designers of Grand Central Terminal. Already skilled in the production of luxury apartment houses, having designed a significant number of them for the New York Central Railroad on Park Avenue just north of the company's terminal building, the firm was hired by developer Michael Paterno.

The Paterno family was known for its conservatively luxurious apartment projects; Michael was a younger member whose ventures usually offered something more, and this cooperative offering fulfilled that expectation. This one might have had still more, however, were it not for a curious little holdout that prevented the expansion of the building site.

Sometime around 1860, a tiny two-story frame house was built at 3 East 83rd Street on a block that was otherwise almost entirely vacant *(Figure 24)*. When the financial panic of 1873 sent real-estate prices plunging, Richard Arnold bought a large portion of the block, including the little white clapboard house. Richard was the son of the founder of the Arnold, Constable & Company dry-goods store.

Well supplied with capital, Arnold built an appropriate new home for himself at the Fifth Avenue corner of his property. As the little cottage was occupied, however, he truncated his own dwelling so as not to disturb the entrenched residents next door. On the other side of the little place he constructed an elegant terrace of brownstone row houses.

Richard Arnold died, his son Hicks Arnold died and Hicks's widow, Harriet Constable Arnold, inherited the clapboard house. In 1924, two elderly spinster sisters were living there and Mrs. Arnold refused to evict them, so Michael Paterno's building site was subject to the same size restriction Richard Arnold had imposed upon himself half a century earlier. To his credit, Paterno not only accepted the holdout graciously, he even altered his construction methods when the excavation blasting frightened the two sisters and broke some of their windowpanes.

Despite the solicitude of Harriet Arnold and Michael Paterno, one of the sisters died three years later, and the other moved out shortly thereafter. The lit-

Figure 24. The 1860s frame cottage at 3 East 83rd Street, photographed about 1929. *(Charles von Urban, courtesy of the Museum of the City of New York.)*

tle house then had a succession of occupants until it was razed in 1953, along with the row of Arnold brownstones, to make way for a blocky and vacuous apartment house that is eminently forgettable.

The structure that arose in 1924 from the excavation adjoining the little white nineteenth-century relic, however, was quite memorable *(Figure 25)*. The original sales brochure described the "truly noble proportions" of 1020 Fifth. It said, "A salon twenty feet wide by forty feet long and eighteen feet high; with a great open fireplace at one end, and three double height windows on Fifth Avenue is a very exceptional room. There are few such rooms in New York. Many of them are in this building."

Besides these grand salons, most of the apartments have a dining room, a library, three large bedrooms and five maids' rooms, plus the customary service and storage spaces. Some apartments omit the extra-height living room and instead are merely conventionally large (with a 32-foot sitting room and a 21-foot master bedroom, both with fireplace). At the first and second floors are two duplex maisonettes, one with a private entry directly from Fifth Avenue. These apartments, too, are spacious and well laid out.

Perhaps the most splendid unit in the building is the top-floor duplex, which augments its grand salon and other large rooms with a stairway to a terraced penthouse at the roof. This encompasses two more master chambers, three additional maids' rooms and a glazed solarium with a serving pantry and a dumbwaiter to the kitchen below—truly a glorious apartment, and with a comparable price tag. In May 1925, while 1020 Fifth Avenue was still under construction, it was bought for $150,000 by Samuel H. Kress, owner of the chain of five-and-ten-cent stores that gave serious competition to Frank W. Woolworth's company. Mrs. Kress still lives there.

The Kress duplex was the most expensive in the building and carried a monthly maintenance charge of $1540 (a figure that could support a small family modestly for an entire year). The other apartments in the building ranged in price from $40,000 to $120,000, with monthly charges from $410 to $1230. For comparison, an apartment in the building sold in 1986 for $4 million. It was then lavishly redecorated for rather more than that figure and featured five years later in *Architectural Digest*.

Figure 25. The newly completed structure at 1020 Fifth Avenue in 1924 with the little holdout cottage adjoining it on the side street. (*Wurts Brothers, courtesy of the Museum of the City of New York.*)

Gracious Gracie
A Resplendent Revolution on East 84th Street at the East River

TEN GRACIE SQUARE was a sign of its times. Completed in 1930, shortly after the city named the easternmost block of East 84th Street Gracie Square, it stands on the site of a modest Italian hospital which in turn was a 1912 conversion of an earlier printing factory. The construction of 10 Gracie reflected the rapid change that took place along East End Avenue in the 1920s.

The transition was certainly dramatic. The area had been devoted to country estates during the eighteenth and early nineteenth centuries, but by the 1880s most of the mansions were given over to other uses (except for Archibald Gracie's house at East 88th Street, which was occupied by the Noah Wheaton family until 1896, and is still standing). The Nathaniel Prime home at East 90th Street, for instance, was subsumed within St. Joseph's Orphan Asylum, and the Jones family mansion at East 82nd Street was replaced by the kind of tenements that soon lined much of East End Avenue (then called Avenue B).

With such changes, industry quickly prospered: John Nesbits's Sons' brick and lime yard was on the south corner of East 80th Street; the Heuber stone works and the Frank Wise Building Materials Company were at East 79th Street; and Fleischmann's Vienna Model Bakery was on the west side of Avenue B at 81st Street, across from a cigar factory and down the street from a coal yard and an ice plant.

In 1928, however, East End Avenue below East 84th Street was restricted to residential buildings, and the area quickly changed to a luxury-apartment enclave. Vincent Astor built several large apartment houses, including 520 and 530 East 86th Street, and 120 East End Avenue, where he lived *(Figure 26)*. In 1928, architects Rosario Candela and William Lawrence Bottomley designed an 89-foot-wide building called One Gracie Square for the corner of East 84th Street and East End, facing Carl Schurz Park *(Figure 27)*.

The most gracious of these newcomers, though, was 10 Gracie Square *(Figure 28)*. Architects Van Wart & Wein, in association with Pleasants Pennington and Albert W. Lewis, working for a syndicate headed by John Drummond Kennedy, concocted several elegant features, the most notable being the entrance. The building boasts what may be New York's only fully covered block-long driveway serving an apartment house. Protected behind locked gates and

controlled by an attendant in an enlarged sentry box, this porte-cochère is wide enough to permit temporary parking on one side with enough room remaining to maneuver a Rolls Royce. Cars can deliver passengers directly to each of three elevator lobbies *(Figure 29)*.

In addition, a private club occupied the floors beneath the elevated street and led out to yacht moorings on the river. (These amenities were doomed when the East River Drive, later named the Franklin D. Roosevelt Drive, was completed in 1942. The docks had to be removed and the club lost its light and views. The space is now devoted to a squash court, a game room and more prosaic uses.)

Achieving such luxury was not easy. The designers faced three towering hurdles: the easterly lot—an entire blockfront between East 83rd and 84th Streets—was set at an angle; maximum advantage had to be taken of the river views *(Figure 30)*, and the builder, T. R. Rhodes Company, had allowed early purchasers to specify room layouts and window placements. The solution: the building met the angled lot line in a series of steps, yielding corner windows and balconies for many of the apartments. Oriel windows enhanced the views from the other units. Possibly to smooth the façade's irregularities and reduce the bulk of the 117-by-200-foot structure, only the corner section was sheathed in limestone, with the flanking portions clad in red brick, making 10 Gracie

Above, left: Figure 26. 120 East End Avenue. *(Irving Underhill, courtesy of the Museum of the City of New York.)*

Above, right: Figure 27. One Gracie Square in a preconstruction artist's rendering. *(Courtesy of Joseph Candela.)*

Above: Figure 28. Ten Gracie Square before the East River Drive cut off its direct access to the water, and in the process also destroyed the little Roman pavilion in Carl Schurz Park. *(Wurts Brothers, courtesy of the Museum of the City of New York.)*

Left, top: Figure 29. The covered driveway and the arcaded entrance to the first of the three elevator lobbies of 10 Gracie Square. *(Wurts Brothers, courtesy of the Museum of the City of New York.)*

Left bottom: Figure 30. Wide-angle waterfront: the view of the East River and the Hellgate railroad bridge from an apartment at 10 Gracie Square. *(Wurts Brothers, courtesy of the Museum of the City of New York.)*

look more like three adjoining buildings rather than one *(Figure 31)*. More than 60 years after it was built, however, the limestone sheathing was cracking and breaking off. Exploratory probes revealed that behind the elegant façade the steelwork that should have supported the stone had inexplicably been left unpainted and unprotected. It had rusted nearly completely away, forcing an expensive reconstruction project. Rustproofing would not have added significantly to the cost, so the question of why it was omitted remains tantalizing.

Complex juggling was needed to accommodate the custom apartment designs, which included 34 duplex and semiduplex suites. In the end, the building contained 42 units ranging from six rooms and three baths, to nineteen rooms and eight baths. The most expensive was a 13-room duplex penthouse that sold originally for $140,000. Perhaps the grandest apartment, however, boasted more space and amenities than most suburban estates. It overlooked Carl Schurz Park and the river and had a 32-by-20-foot living room, a balcony fronting on the river, three working fireplaces, a graceful curving staircase at the end of a 31-foot entrance gallery, seven bedrooms, a dining room, a library and servants' quarters.

Such opulence later attracted a host of celebrities: conductors André Kostelanetz and Leopold Stokowski; the former Mrs. Stokowski—Gloria Vanderbilt—who returned to the building 30 years after the couple moved out; journalist and critic Alexander Woollcott, who remained at 10 Gracie until he died in 1943; publishers John Fairchild and Horace Havemeyer III; and singer Lily Pons.

Ten Gracie's real claim on history is that it helped usher in an era. Since 1930, the area around East End Avenue has been a sanctuary for families. First

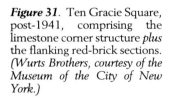

Figure 31. Ten Gracie Square, post-1941, comprising the limestone corner structure *plus* the flanking red-brick sections. *(Wurts Brothers, courtesy of the Museum of the City of New York.)*

came the Chapin School, followed closely by Brearley. Add in the recreational attractions of Carl Schurz Park and the allure of the river, and you have a stronghold where families and large apartments continue to prosper.

Ten Gracie Square perhaps refined the automobile entrance in New York, but it was not the first of its kind. Grand mansions of nineteenth-century New York had portes-cochères where visitors could alight from their carriages under cover. Some, such as the expanded house of Cornelius Vanderbilt II at West 58th Street and Fifth Avenue, also included a private driveway to protect guests from gaping *hoi polloi.*

Portes-cochères at many of the earliest apartment houses were recessed into the building fronts and were fully open to view. The covered driveway at the Montana Apartments at 375 Park Avenue was demolished more than 30 years ago, while a similar one in the Wyoming at West 55th Street and Seventh Avenue was converted even earlier to provide streetfront store space.

Still remaining, however, is the porte-cochère at 440 Riverside Drive, a space so elegantly detailed that the arrival of anything less than an Aston Martin or a Daimler would be a sacrilege *(Figure 32)*. Also still in existence, but blocked off and unused, is the covered entrance driveway of the Langham at 135 Central Park West *(Figure 33)*. The horse-drawn two-wheeled hansom cab shown in an early publicity drawing of the driveway was a common form of public transportation in 1905, when the building opened.

Figure 33. The disused carriage entry at 135 Central Park West in an early publicity rendering. *(Collection of Andrew Alpern.)*

In the 1920s, One and Two Sutton Place South established a precedent of covered driveways at large apartment houses adjacent to the East River, but the scale of their automotive entries *(Figure 34)* pales in comparison to that of Ten Gracie.

Figure 34. The entrance driveway of One Sutton Place South in 1926, designed by Rosario Candela. *(Wurts Brothers, courtesy of the Museum of the City of New York.)*

Joyful Jacobethan

Musical Inspiration at 1025 Park Avenue

FROM 1903, WHEN the electrification of the underground railroad trains was announced, until after World War I, when apartment-house living began to flower, Park Avenue boasted many one-family residences. One of the few such houses that remain—and perhaps the most unusual—is 1025 Park Avenue *(Figure 35)*.

Designed by John Russell Pope, the architect of the Jefferson Memorial and the National Gallery in Washington, and the Roosevelt Memorial wing of New York's Museum of Natural History, the 1913 mansion was an "interpretation" of several different English country houses of the Elizabethan and Jacobean periods. Dubbed "Jacobethan" by the somewhat supercilious architectural critics of the day, the style worked well on its constricted mid-block site.

The plan integrated the disparate rooms, ceilings, paneling and other interior elements imported from Europe by Reginald and Anna De Koven, the wealthy and much-traveled owners. Reginald began in banking in Chicago, but late in the nineteenth century moved his venue to New York and changed his vocation to music. Financially successful and immensely popular, he wrote many operas and operettas, as well as several hundred songs, piano pieces and orchestral suites, and also found time to be music critic for the *New York World*, the *New York Journal* and *Harper's Weekly*. His wife was equally successful as a writer, producing fiction, histories, translations and, in 1926, an autobiography.

The De Kovens were similarly accomplished on the social scene, mounting grand soirées and regular musicales. The centerpiece of these affairs was their home's grand second-floor two-storied drawing room. It was 27 feet wide and nearly 60 feet long, with a baronial fireplace at one end and a carved minstrels' gallery at the other. Working in conjunction with this was a paneled and book-lined library, three ground-floor reception rooms and a huge connecting stair hall modeled on the one at Knole, in Kent, England.

The De Kovens lived and entertained in this splendid residence only during the opera season. They spent the rest of the year at houses in Washington, Newport and Italy. Reginald De Koven died in 1920; Anna later left for her retreat in Maine and died there in 1953 at age 92, but the house remained in the family only through World War II.

In 1945, following the death of daughter Ethel De Koven Hudson, a syndicate of investors bought the mansion and converted it into a multifamily apartment house. As part of the rehabilitation, the grandiose ballroom was split horizontally into two floors, and then cut again to form four separate rooms that were still large by ordinary apartment standards. The other rooms were sensitively reworked to form modest simplex and duplex units of considerable character. A later owner restored much of the deteriorated portions of the original interior and converted the building to a cooperative in 1959.

The apartments have changed hands infrequently, and prices are high: a two-bedroom duplex incorporating the original library as its sitting room was listed at $1 million in 1991, a time considered by many to have been the bottom of the market for such apartments. By comparison, when the daughter's estate sold the house, the entire 25-room structure had been assessed at $210,000, including the land.

Figure 35. The De Koven residence in 1913. The grand drawing room spanned the full width of the house at the second floor. *(Courtesy of the Museum of the City of New York.)*

Haute Hampshire

From False Starts to Hotel to Home at 150 Central Park South

HAMPSHIRE HOUSE IS a luxurious Central Park South cooperative with expansive suites and the services of a well-tended hotel. Apartments there are not cheap: In 1990 Sotheby's offered a one-bedroom unit for $850,000 (with a monthly maintenance charge of $2200); five years earlier a two-bedroom terraced suite sold for $1.6 million. Yet it was not always so. New Yorkers with long memories will recall that all 37 stories sat vacant and unfinished for six years during the Great Depression of the 1930s.

The story began during the heady boom of the late 1920s, when nearly anything old fell to the demolition ball and new buildings were finished almost before the ink dried on the architects' drawings. In 1926, plans were filed for a cooperative apartment hotel called the Meurice. Slated for the easternmost section of the old Navarro Apartments site *(Figure 36)*, the hotel was to extend through the block from West 58th to 59th Streets, midway between Sixth and Seventh Avenues.

One of the eight Navarro buildings was torn down early in 1927, and the first section of the Meurice went up at 145 West 58th Street. Completed in 1929, the 13-story residential hotel was designed in a modified Georgian style by architects Caughey & Evans. In an interview several years ago with architecture historian Christopher Gray, A. Rollin Caughey's son revealed that the unbuilt West 59th Street section had been designed to contain medical offices and apartments in a slender tower topped with a streamlined dome. After the stock-market crash, however, Caughey redesigned 150 West 59th Street as a more eclectic structure with setback terraces and a huge ridge roof with end hips *(Figure 37)*. He filed new plans in January 1931, and the work was commenced by the H. K. Ferguson Company of Cleveland, in conjunction with Eugene E. Lignante. By March, the steel structure was well along and brickwork reached the eighth floor.

On March 25, Caughey held a grand cornerstone-laying ceremony for the $6 million project. Inside the cornerstone block was an assemblage of artifacts asserted to represent "the modern spirit in art, literature, and science": photographs of Thomas Hart Benton's murals at the New School for Social Research; the musical score to *Skyscrapers* by John Alden Carpenter; copies of Hemingway's *A Farewell to Arms* and O'Neill's *Strange Interlude*; and special

Figure 36. The Navarro Apartments in 1886, the site on which the Hampshire House opened half a century later. *(Courtesy of The New-York Historical Society.)*

rag editions of each of New York's daily newspapers. Because the building's architecture supposedly recalled the old homes of the county of Hampshire in England, the hotel's new name, Hampshire House, was chiseled into the cornerstone, along with the legend, "Dedicated to Yesterday's Charm and Tomorrow's Convenience," and the date, 1931.

Construction proceeded rapidly, with nearly three-quarters completed by the middle of June. Then, quite abruptly, the contractor walked off the job. The New York Title and Mortgage Company, which had already advanced $2.2 million of a $3 million loan to the builders, foreclosed on its lien, boarded up the windows and doors, and hired a guard to stand watch. The mortgage company was itself placed into receivership in 1933, its three court-appointed trustees being assigned the unenviable task of trying to liquidate the Hampshire House—a vain prospect with the country's deepening economic malaise and the city's prospects for recovery dark. The best offer came in November 1936, when Simon F. Rifkind, then law partner of Senator Robert F. Wagner and later senior partner of Paul Weiss, Rifkind, Wharton & Garrison, offered $800,000 with a ten percent deposit. The trustees rejected the bid, and on December 30, 1936, announced that they would complete Hampshire House themselves as a rental apartment hotel.

The Guaranty Trust Company advanced a building loan of $1.5 million, Douglas E. Elliman & Co. was retained as managing agent, and the original architect, A. Rollin Caughey, was hired to alter and finish the building. Besides attending to six years of weathering and deterioration, Caughey subdivided some of the larger upper-floor apartments. In its reworked form, Hampshire House had suites of one to seven rooms, and four gracious duplexes at the top.

Since the interior design was important for marketing the building, the bondholders' trustees hired Dorothy Draper, an eclectically original and highly successful decorator. With a $15,000 fee, a $400,000 budget and a five-month deadline, she and her staff designer, Lester Grundy, melded overscale plaster

Figure 37. Hampshire House, ca. 1960. *(Courtesy of Christopher Gray)*

interpretations of Grinling Gibbons' seventeenth-century carvings, Art Deco and Victorian—a mixture that, in lesser hands, would have been a disaster. A muralist painted bunches of huge cabbage roses on some of the common-area walls and reproduced the design on glazed chintz for the bedrooms. The main dining room's minimalist glass wall opened onto a garden courtyard, laid out with trees, flowers and a fountain—all of which were reflected in a fully mirrored wall at the opposite side of the dining room. Draper's work was appreciated enough by the managing agent that he gave her a 30 percent discount off the rent on one of the upper-floor duplexes.

The Hampshire House rented well following its October 1937 opening, and weathered the end of the Depression and the war years. Late in 1945, Arnold S. Kirkeby, a large-scale hotel operator from Chicago, offered to buy the property. The deal was closed in January 1946 for $3.5 million. Kirkeby ran the hotel for three years, converting it to cooperative ownership in 1949.

In contrast to the comprehensive and well-regulated prospectuses we expect today, this co-op offering plan provided the barest minimum of information to purchasers. Prices ranged from $5100 for a studio (plus $110 per month for maintenance) to $39,900 for a terraced three-bedroom duplex (monthly maintenance of $865). A maid's room could be had for $900, with a monthly charge of $19.50. The cooperative corporation retained twelve small apartments for income. The management rented these out, along with temporarily vacant apartments. This continued until 1972, when the organization was converted to a straight cooperative, but with hotel services. The building is now flourishing as a luxury apartment house with dining facilities and housekeeping services, a hearty sign that not all ghosts remain incorporeal *(Figure 38)*.

Hampshire House was not the only building in New York to stand vacant—the 22-story structure at the northwest corner of West 72nd Street and West End Avenue remained empty and unfinished for more than 17 years *(Figure 39)*.

Begun in 1923, it was intended to be a combination hotel and hospital and was expected to cost more than $3 million. An investment group put up that sum, but as completion neared and additional money was needed, management was unable to come up with an extra $500,000. In 1927, a new group bought the unfinished project, expecting to complete it as a "$5,000,000 national cancer hospital." That plan also fell through.

Investor Sumner Gerard bought the vacant structure at a 1932 foreclosure sale for $200,000, and resold it in 1938. In 1940, the city took possession for unpaid taxes, and sold it at auction the following year for $413,000. The buyer defaulted, however, and the property was reauctioned. Ultimately, it was finished as an apartment house, but not before it had etched itself into the minds of many West Siders as a symbol of the dangers of real-estate speculation.

More recently, the former Gotham Hotel at West 55th Street and Fifth Avenue was boarded up for several years—the result of an eccentric vision of the hotel of the future, gone spectacularly awry *(Figure 40)*. Swiss entrepreneur René Hatt thought guests at a chic luxury hotel would appreciate purple marble bathtubs—in the bedrooms, directly adjoining the beds. He was convinced that a color scheme of burgundy and black walls with violet carpets would be *comme il faut*. He and his partners poured $100 million into the Gotham, but were forced to shutter the project when it became evident that they would need at least another $40 million to finish it to Hatt's taste. Ultimately the unused marble baths were torn out and the building was reconstructed and reopened as a more conventional hotel.

In 1985, Jacopo Finkelstein constructed a 46-story building at 135 West 52nd Street that was to be a condominium for "the sometime New Yorker." He

Figure 38. The dual entrances to Hampshire House in 1988. *(Andrew Alpern.)*

touted it as the ultimate home-away-from-home for jet-setting repeat visitors, and called his venture The Manhattan *(Figure 41)*. Amenities included an office/conference facility, a health club, multilingual concierge services and prices to match. Trouble was, the apartment layouts were cramped and mean, and the building's façade looked like a maximum security prison. Five years later, the building was still completely vacant, and Finkelstein was still in prison (for shady financial dealings which may or may not have involved the building).

In 1981, a group of foreign investors headed by an Egyptian, Dr. Gamil Ghaleb, bought a vacant five-story tenement house at 813 Park Avenue *(Figure 42)*. The group added five more floors plus a penthouse, and converted the interiors into strange apartments that could not sell. Kitchens were too small, so refrigerators were installed in living rooms; master bedrooms served as corridors to second bedrooms. Eventually the building was boarded up, and the investors walked away from several million wasted dollars. It remained vacant

Above, left: Figure 39. 265 West End Avenue ca. 1945, having been reconstructed as an apartment house. *(Courtesy of Christopher Gray.)*

Above, right: Figure 40. The Gotham Hotel at Fifth Avenue and West 55th Street, ca. 1908. *(Wurts Brothers, courtesy of the Museum of the City of New York and Christopher Gray.)*

Below: Figure 41. 135 West 52nd Street as originally conceived. *(Collection of Andrew Alpern.)*

Right: Figure 42. 813 Park Avenue while still a five-story tenement house, ca. 1940. *(Courtesy of the New York City Municipal Archives and Christopher Gray.)*

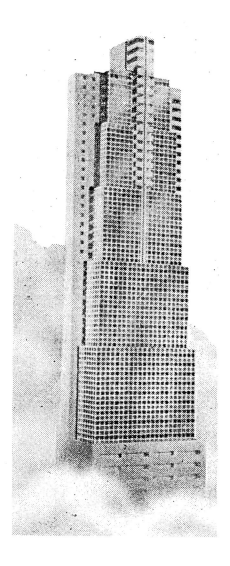

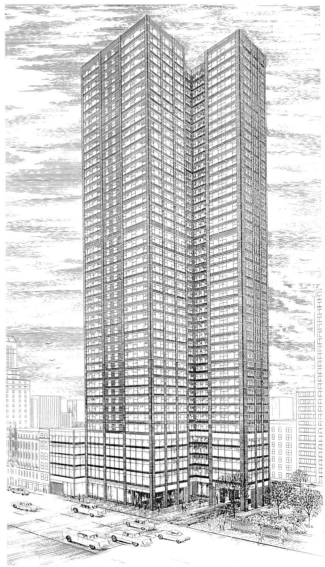

until 1990, when new owners reconstructed it. With altered floor levels to afford extra-height living rooms, the third incarnation of the building provided three stacked quadruplexes, each with a private elevator *(Figure 43)*. Offered with tenancy-in-common ownership, the project avoided the regulatory scrutiny of the more conventional co-op or condominium ownership plan. Unit prices were set at $5 million, but were reduced when the market proved resistant. Then, in 1995, the entire building—18,000 square feet—was offered at $7.5 million . . . as a "rare opportunity for investment or large family."

The Sheffield Apartments on West 57th Street was also shuttered and fenced off when its original builder went bankrupt. Rose Associates finished the structure in 1979, six years after it had been started *(Figure 44)*.

Above, left: Figure 43. The erstwhile tenement at 813 Park Avenue, reconstructed as stacked town houses for three families. *(Courtesy of Michael Goldstein.)*

Above, right: Figure 44. The Sheffield at 322 West 57th Street as presented in a publicity brochure. *(Rendering by Duc Tjein.)*

Picturesque Pomander

Apartments in a Pseudo Stage Set on the Upper West Side

POMANDER WALK IS about as far from the ordinary as New York City living can get. Erected in 1921 by Thomas Healy, an Irish immigrant restaurateur, this grouping of 27 two- and three-story houses, standing mid-block between Broadway and West End Avenue and running from West 94th to 95th Streets, was a free interpretation of the stage set for a Broadway play, which in turn was a romanticized vision of an English village from the time of King George III *(Figure 45)*. And that's just part of the story.

The original Pomander Walk was part of the village of Chiswick by the Thames. It became the setting and title for a novel and then a three-act comedy, which had a successful stint in London and a 12-week run at New York's Wallack's Theatre late in 1910. Healy, charmed by the play's crescent of little houses, recreated the set on his leased Manhattan site. Although the buildings, designed by architects Beverly King and Shiras Campbell, were more sixteenth-century Tudor than eighteenth-century classical, the theatrical inspiration was obvious. Besides the rough stone-and-brick walls, shrubbery and flower beds, it had an intimate scale that shut out its urban surroundings *(Figure 46)*.

This romantic enclave, however, was a developer's nightmare: Construction costs and operating expenses of the low-density project eliminated profit. It was barely kept alive by Healy's adjoining project, the old Astor Model Market at the corner of West 95th Street and Broadway *(Figure 47)*. Healy bought the huge, low, arcaded market in 1917. He enhanced it with an indoor ice-skating rink and turned some of the stalls into retail and office space. He also created a first-floor theater that eventually became Symphony Space, and a lower-level restaurant, Sunken Gardens, which was replaced in 1931 by a movie theater called the Thalia. For two generations, the tickets sold to its foreign films and revivals helped Pomander Walk escape the wrecker's ball.

By 1980, after the Thalia had closed and the Healy properties ceased being profitable, the market and Pomander Walk faced demolition. Pomander's rent-controlled tenantry tried to ward off doom by turning to the city's Landmarks Preservation Commission, which could prevent any new development by designating the enclave a landmark. In September 1982, after much posturing and

Figure 45. Enter, stage left. Did Dorothy and Lillian Gish, Humphrey Bogart and Rosalind Russell live here along Pomander Walk? *(Architecture and Building, courtesy of Christopher Gray.)*

Figure 46. Pomander Walk's entrance from the street, in the days before the changing neighborhood necessitated locked safety gates. *(Architecture and Building, courtesy of Christopher Gray.)*

politicking and two public hearings, the tenants won. Citing the "delightful architectural whimsy" of the development, the commission's report observed: "One of the impressive features of Pomander Walk is its skillful use of landscape elements. On this narrow pedestrian street the small-scale houses are set behind individual miniature hedges and flowerbeds, creating a tranquil, secluded, livable environment—a startling contrast to the bustle of nearby Broadway."

The little colony lives on, and so do the legends. One is that each of the houses was originally a single-family cottage, when, in fact, they have remained

essentially unchanged from their tiny one- and two-bedroom-apartment lay-outs, one on each floor. Another is that the cast of theatrical tenants has in-cluded Dorothy and Lillian Gish, Humphrey Bogart and Rosalind Russell. The facts: Miss Lillian said that she never lived there, and the two other associa-tions may well be similarly apocryphal (although about half the residents at the time of its cooperative conversion were connected in one way or another with the arts). Believe what you want, but rest assured, with a history like Pomander Walk's, almost anything goes.

Figure 47. The Astor Market at West 95th Street and Broadway, a model public-market project erected by Vincent Astor and opened in 1915. *(Courtesy of the Museum of the City of New York and Christopher Gray.)*

What Once Was on West End

The Grander Days of 401 West End Avenue

MANY OF THE West SIDE buildings that were converted to cooperative status relatively recently offer good value in small apartments. Formerly, such accommodations could be had only if a relative died, because of the peculiarities of the rent-control laws. Quite a few of these are in buildings whose earlier incarnations were very different from what is now to be seen, many dating to the early 1900s.

At the turn of the century, there was a tremendous optimism that the succeeding 100 years would be vastly better than the years just past. The Spanish–American War was over, there had not been a financial panic for several years and even Queen Victoria, who had finally come out of mourning for Prince Albert, was enthusiastic about the future.

Closer to home, the sidewalks of West End Avenue had been planted with trees and plots of grass, and elegant new apartment houses were being erected. The income tax of the Civil War days was long forgotten; undiminished use of increasing incomes was expected for the indefinite future by the expanding middle class.

Into this oasis of endless opportunity stepped William B. Franke, a real-estate entrepreneur who served himself as a combination architect, builder and owner, and who had been designing buildings since 1875. He bought a site at the northwest corner of West End Avenue and West 79th Street that was encumbered only with a very modest three-story frame house. Franke took the old building down and replaced it with a substantial nine-story apartment house that incorporated the most imaginative and up-to-date features for attracting tenants that he could muster. In the spirit of the times, he named it the New Century and promoted it heavily.

Franke's new building was an impressive pile *(Figure 48)*. An elegant composition of gray limestone and red brick, it was separated from the sidewalk by a dry-moat areaway that brought light to the billiard room and the additional servants' quarters he provided in the basement. The entrance on the avenue was highlighted and protected by an elaborate porch supported on four Ionic columns and topped with a balustraded railing. Similar balustrades adorned the

Figure 48. The New Century Apartments at West 79th Street and West End Avenue in 1901. The building remains, but gone are the columned porch, the trees, grass plots and the splendidly spiky cornice. *(Irving Underhill, courtesy of the Museum of the City of New York.)*

decorative balconies on the two primary elevations of the building, and the entire structure was crowned with a magnificent metal cornice that superimposed dentil moldings, floriated console brackets and lions' heads, and was surmounted by Greek antefixae embellished with anthemia.

Within, each floor had two apartments, each of ten or 11 rooms and three baths. Well in advance of the age, the layouts clustered the entertaining suite of parlor, library and dining room around an entrance hall at the front of each apartment, with the private sleeping quarters in a separate wing to the back. The detailing was lavish, with parquet floors and polished woodwork, recessed sliding doors and coffered ceilings.

A fireproof safe was installed in the wall of each master bedroom, fireproof construction was used throughout, and water entering the building from the city's mains was filtered before being piped to the apartments. A central refrigeration plant serviced cold-storage facilities in each kitchen, with an additional cold-storage room in the basement for each apartment. Also in the basement were individual trunk rooms for each unit, as well as wine cellars.

An especially unusual feature was the two-story annex adjoining on West 79th Street. Its basement housed the boilers and other mechanical equipment for the building, thus giving greater quiet and safety to the residents in the main structure. The ground floor of the annex provided storage for electric automobiles, "a great attraction for people who indulge in the luxury," according to the promotional material. Also at that level was a charging room for the necessary automobile batteries, and on the second floor was a fully equipped steam laundry for the use of the building's tenants. In a move that antedated the Hertz Company by a quarter of a century, William Franke offered automobiles "of different styles" for rent to his tenants "at reasonable rates." "Such a vehicle can be made ready at a few minutes' notice," he asserted.

The luxurious living style which the building represented did not survive the Great Depression, and in 1935 the Excelsior Savings Bank foreclosed on the mortgage. The bank was faced with the same depressed market for large apartments that had thwarted the building's prior owner, but it had the advantage of ready cash to invest in an alteration that might return the building to a viable financial condition. Using the services of architect Joseph M. Berlinger, the bank reconstructed the interior to create seven small apartments on each floor.

Electric automobiles had only a brief period of popularity, and the two-story annex had been converted earlier to use as a commercial garage. In 1942, it was reconverted and dedicated as a synagogue. The Orthodox Congregation Kehilath Jacob moved in, as did its rabbi, who lived in an apartment upstairs, constructed in what had formerly been the steam laundry.

Half a century later, the congregation still occupies the annex, with the upstairs apartment converted to its offices following the rabbi's death in 1994. However, the columned porch is gone from the main apartment building, the splendid cornice is gone from the top of the structure and the way of life the New Century once catered to is a mere memory. What remains, nonetheless, is the continuing need of New Yorkers for shelter, with 401 West End continuing to provide 50 families with accommodations.

Risky San Remo

The Best and Worst of Times on Central Park West

THE SAN REMO, one of Central Park West's grandest apartment houses, was a textbook case of poor timing. Completed a year after the stock-market crash in 1929, it barely weathered the cold realities of the Great Depression.

Indeed, its developers unwittingly followed a recipe for disaster. They set out to replace the old San Remo, one of several "family" hotels on Central Park West *(Figure 49)*. Erected in sections in the late nineteenth century, it had ten stories, two canopied entrances on Central Park West and a pair of rudimentary towers. By the late 1920s, the hotel's ponderous Romanesque architecture and primitive planning were hopelessly out of date.

HRH Construction Corporation, which had recently completed the Beresford at Central Park West and West 81st Street, did not see the country's impending financial morass and set its standards high. They bought five brownstone row houses adjoining the hotel, which stood between West 74th and 75th Streets, enlarging the property to about 31,000 square feet *(Figure 50)*. This qualified it for special treatment under the 1929 Multiple Dwelling Law and allowed architect Emery Roth to design a 27-story building—one of the tallest residential structures in the city at the time. The first of four twin-towers ultimately constructed on Central Park West, it was a dramatic presence on the skyline *(Figure 51)*.

Roth also concentrated on detail. The first three floors of the San Remo's 17-story base are rusticated limestone, and the rest is buff-colored brick with ornamental terra-cotta. Classical balustrades, pediments and cartouches enliven the façade and accentuate the upper-floor setbacks, providing a logical transition to the towers, which are masterly amalgams of Greek, Roman and Baroque styles. The ten-story shafts start out quite simply, but bloom into increasing animation towards the tops with volutes, rosettes, broken pediments, garlands and huge urns that aesthetically support circular *tempietti* at the crown. The design source for these little temples was the Choragic Monument of Lysicrates, erected in Athens in 334 B.C. The original had a brazier atop its conical roof to hold a memorial flame, and in a translation to twentieth-century use, each of Roth's dual versions has a copper lantern at its pinnacle, providing a lighted

Figure 49. The old San Remo hotel in its fully expanded form. It had been erected in sections in the late nineteenth century by Michael Brennan to designs of Edward Angell. *(Joseph Byron, courtesy of the Museum of the City of New York.)*

Below: Figure 50. Central Park West as it looked in 1912 when it was dominated by family hotels, institutional structures and relatively low apartment houses. *(Irving Underhill, courtesy of the Museum of the City of New York.)*

Left: Figure 51. The San Remo early in the Depression: proudly tall and stately, but economically battered by its many vacant apartments. *(Wurts Brothers, courtesy of the Museum of the City of New York.)*

beacon 400 feet above the pavement *(Figure 52)*. The two towers of the new San Remo echoed (in vastly grander form) the stumpy pyramidal towers of its eponymous predecessor, and the pair of canopied entrances to the nineteenth-century hotel were duplicated in corresponding entry portals to its twentieth-century reincarnation. By separating the entrances and providing two entrance lobbies, Roth was able to offer the luxury of small elevator halls that serve only two apartments per landing on the upper floors.

Despite such elegance and thoughtful planning, the building remained one-third vacant a year after it opened. The bank that held the mortgage collapsed, and the bank's officers were charged with having taken too speculative a risk in backing the San Remo, thereby violating their fiduciary duty to their depositors. A succession of owners tried to create financial stability—first by lowering the rents and then by subdividing many of the apartments to create more marketable units—but each went bankrupt. The ultimate humiliation came in 1940, when the Beresford and the San Remo were together sold for a mere $25,000 in cash over the existing mortgages.

Much more than money was lost, however. Carving the building into 142 apartments in place of the original 122 eliminated many unique spaces. The

Figure 52. A dual crescendo of architectural ornamentation atop the San Remo's twin towers. *(Andrew Alpern.)*

units had ranged from six to 16 rooms. Even the smallest was exceptionally spacious, and all were planned around central foyers—a Roth signature touch. Each master bedroom had a bathroom and generous closet space, and every living room had a fireplace. Ceilings were set at a lofty 11 feet, and were constructed on a suspended wire-lath armature, eliminating aesthetically restricting beam drops. Most floors of the base section comprised seven apartments of six to 11 rooms.

The larger units were at the terraced setback floors and in the southern tower, which originally contained 14-room duplexes, each with seven baths and a powder room. The lower levels of these suites boasted 22-by-35-foot living rooms, 17-foot-by-24-foot dining rooms, 20-foot libraries and 17-foot breakfast rooms. Curved staircases swept past windows overlooking Central Park and led to upper levels with four master bedrooms. There were five maids' rooms and a back stairs. Because of the tower's irregular shape, these apartments had 360-degree views, with three exposures in the living rooms. Rents reached $21,000 a year at a time when a certified public accountant was considered successful at an annual income of $2500.

After World War II, the luxury-apartment market rebounded and the San Remo found solid footing. It prospered despite the "temporary" wartime rent-control regulations (still hamstringing landlords half a century later) and was later converted to a cooperative by its residents. Like many West Side buildings, it has provided long-time homes for successful merchants and professionals. It has also been a mecca for such luminaries of the performing arts as Eddie Cantor, Barry Manilow, Dustin Hoffman, Diane Keaton, Tony Randall and Mary Tyler Moore, as well as a Pulitzer Prize–winning architecture critic of the *New York Times*. Of course, apartments are not cheap: A lower-floor 11-room unit sold at the height of the 1987 boom for $4.6 million.

In 1987 the San Remo was officially designated by the city's Landmarks Preservation Commission and was then restored to near-new condition. Despite its rocky beginnings, it stands as a testament to good design.

Neo-Luxury Normandy

140 Riverside Drive Marked the End of the Depression

TOWERING ABOVE RIVERSIDE Drive, the Normandy is a link between the grand apartment houses of the 1920s and the drab boxes of the postwar 1940s and 1950s. Designed in 1938, that brief moment when the dark days of the Depression seemed to be over and the imminence of a worldwide war had not yet been fully perceived, it is both a survival of an earlier approach to apartments and a precursor of today's tightly planned multifamily towers.

By the spring of 1938, the world was pulling itself out of the Great Depression. Optimism was only slightly tempered by the ominous portents of war rumbling in Europe, and America's construction industry was again beginning to flex its muscles. The heady mood of the 1920s was gone, but buildings were still needed, and architects took pencils in hand. The more imaginative ones—such as the notable Emery Roth—were both designers and developers, and their lavish plans symbolized a nation pulling out of disaster.

The area that Roth and his partners chose for their project was one of the city's lushest. With its handsome park, cool river zephyrs and expansive views of the Hudson and New Jersey, Riverside Drive was envisioned as being the premier boulevard of the city. Riverside Park was introduced in a small promotional pamphlet in 1865 that suggested an ornamental landscape was an appropriate treatment for the craggy western border of Manhattan north of West 72nd Street. Championed by the protean civic activist Andrew Haswell Green, the legislation authorizing the new park became law on April 24, 1867. Plans were prepared by Frederick Law Olmsted for a linear landscape bordered by a distinctly nonlinear Riverside Drive. The necessary land acquisitions were completed by 1872, and the finished Park and Drive opened in 1880.

Unlike the East Side, where most of the millionaires' mansions were built, the Drive was developed primarily as a street of apartment houses—apart from the chateauesque Schwab mansion at West 73rd Street and a number of comfortable large houses for the prosperous middle class. The blockfront between West 86th and 87th Streets was also an exception. Eight handsome but modest row houses were erected there in 1896 by the architect/builder Henry Cook *(Figure 53)*. A scant 25 years later, Dr. John A. Harriss bought the property

Figure 53. Riverside Drive, north from West 86th Street, ca. 1925, showing the eight row houses erected in 1896 by Henry Cook. *(Courtesy of The New-York Historical Society.)*

and proposed to erect a "high-grade apartment house." He never did, however, and in 1933 he lost his investment to a mortgage foreclosure.

The row houses, along with one adjoining on West 86th Street and three more on West 87th, made a substantial site that could carry a status address of 140 Riverside Drive. Adding to its desirability was the convenience of the nearby Broadway subway stop, multiple bus lines serving the immediate area, and the recreational terraces of the Soldiers' and Sailors' Monument. An extra impetus was the removal of a significant eyesore when Riverside Park was rebuilt in 1937 to hide the railroad tracks that blocked access to the waterside.

Emery Roth was sensitive to the changes wrought by the Depression. The concept of a luxury apartment in the 1920s included plenty of space, lavish fitments and many servants. In the 1930s, such apartments were difficult to rent and many of the largest were subdivided into smaller, more marketable units. Roth's own San Remo on Central Park West was partially altered in this manner not long after it opened in 1930 and before it could be fully rented.

The economic recovery toward the end of the decade spurred the need for a new kind of luxury housing. In addition, the New York World's Fair was to open in April 1939, and Emery Roth wanted his new project to carry its spirit of hope and change. The building was dubbed the Normandy, perhaps to reflect the prestige of the French luxury liner, the *Normandie*, which had been hailed as the last word in Art Deco elegance and classical comfort. (The ship made its maiden voyage in 1935, and its hundredth crossing in 1938, just a few weeks before the plans for the Normandy were filed with the city's Department of Buildings. In February 1942, shortly after the Japanese attack on Pearl Harbor, the *Normandie* burned at its pier on the Hudson. It had been seized by the United States after Germany occupied France and was destroyed while being converted for use as a troopship.)

Roth approached the design of the new Normandy apartment house on several fronts. He began with a traditional Beaux-Arts plan, creating an H-shaped structure that provided corner or floor-through orientations for all but the smallest units. There were 15 apartments on a typical floor served by two elevator banks, each accessed from the block-long lobby that stretched from West 86th to 87th Streets. Although the apartments were dramatically smaller than those considered luxurious a decade earlier, they were thoughtfully designed, reflecting an earlier graciousness. A three-bedroom unit that in 1928 would have included four baths, two maids' rooms and a large dining room, now had but two baths, no servants' quarters and a modest dining alcove adjoining the foyer. There were exceptionally small one-bedroom suites and studios without separate bedrooms—most unusual for a luxury building. Nonetheless, some of the apartments had such distinctive touches as semicircular dining bays off the living rooms, large round foyers, curved corner windows (which enabled expanded views to substitute for expansive space) and small corner and setback terraces for a number of upper floor units.

The building's outward appearance provided a curious study in contrasts— an odd mixture of traditional and new, lavish and spare. Roth borrowed certain themes from his previous projects *(Figure 54)*. The Normandy featured rudimentary versions of the San Remo's twin towers, with similar enlarged corner piers, broken-pedimented enframements and beacon lights at the top. But where the predecessor's towers incorporated soaring elaborate circular temples, these had simpler ridge roofs with end hips.

Roth recalled his other Central Park West apartment house, the Beresford, with stone obelisks at the corners of the penthouse roof level and upper-floor

Figure 54. The Normandy as depicted in an artist's publicity rendering. *(Courtesy of Emery Roth & Sons, Architects.)*

stone balustrades to emphasize the Italian Renaissance flavor of the building. At ground level, similar balustrades and stone urns continued that feeling, tempered with a completely different design approach—the simplified and streamlined version of Art Deco known as Art Moderne. The style was evident in the cantilevered corners, the curved windows and the horizontal banding—banding that was a modern interpretation of the rustication common to so many of the apartment houses of the 1920s—at the two-storied limestone base section.

The banding turned the corners of the Normandy and continued around a recessed garden courtyard in the center of the Riverside Drive frontage. This unusual feature was a logical outgrowth of the placement of the two building entrances on the side streets, leaving the park side free. Perhaps inadvertently, this arrangement recalls the 1923 design of the Georgian-styled apartment house at 655 Park Avenue *(see pages 36–40)*. The Normandy mirrors the earlier plan in its side-street entrances, its recessed garden courtyard on the avenue, its horizontal limestone rustication and even in its curved corners. The two buildings represent dramatically different worlds, yet their affinity is striking.

Emery Roth "explained" the apparent contradiction of having a modern building that incorporated classical details and forms. In the *New York Sun* in 1938, he wrote:

> It will be definitely 1939. That doesn't mean "modernistic." Every building is ultra modern when erected, whether it is inspired by any one of the historic periods of architecture or whether it is planned with a conscious search for originality. Architecture of all periods and at all times was modern for its particular era. I am fond of so-called old Italian architecture. If today I designed a building of old Italian architecture, it would emerge nevertheless as a modern structure, always to be recognized as of 1939.

Noted as a particularly important link in the architectural chain, the Normandy was designated in 1985 as an official landmark by New York City's Landmarks Preservation Commission. According to the Commission's report, the "last of the great Upper West Side apartment houses from the era of its most intense development, the Normandy reflects, in its unusual cross of Italian Renaissance and Moderne, the two main design currents of that inter-war period."

Highly visible, beautifully designed and still largely intact, the building symbolizes the grand era of twentieth-century urbanism, and is a true landmark of the Upper West Side.

Prewar Pioneer

Technological Innovation at 25 East 83rd Street

As THE GREAT Depression receded, New York City architecture experienced several breakthroughs—building design became "Moderne," technology brought undreamed-of comforts, and 25 East 83rd Street was completed *(Figure 55)*.

Opened in 1938, this dramatically innovative apartment house was a sort of socioeconomic experiment conducted by architect Frederick Lee Ackerman and his consulting engineer, Sullivan A. S. Patorno. Ackerman was an authority on the special needs of mass housing, writing extensively on the subject and helping the federal government to deal with the housing crises of both world wars. As befitted the still-constrained economy of the late 1930s, he designed 25 East 83rd Street to provide modestly compact apartments of two to four rooms.

Although short on space (at least by the standards of the luxury buildings of the 1920s), these apartments were long on creature comforts. The building's most unusual feature was its central air-conditioning system—the first for a New York apartment house. This complex system provided individual controls in each apartment, enabling one suite to be heated as another was cooled, with an individually adjusted internal water spray that humidified the air. Each apartment had separate summer and winter thermostats, and two central equipment rooms were located on every floor.

The greatest innovation, however, was the system's use of mechanically cooled condenser water rather than city-supplied cold water. Anticipating the widespread use of central air-conditioning (something that did not happen for another quarter-century), this feature drew favorable mention in the *Real Estate Record*, a trade journal: "According to the latest available figures on water consumption in New York City, it may be only a few years until the situation reaches a point where all air-conditioning systems will be required to use cooling towers to conserve the city's water supply."

Because the building had a master meter and paid lower electricity rates, Ackerman provided the luxury of electric stoves and refrigerators (gas was more customarily used to fuel both these appliances), and installed electric heaters in each bathroom. He rejected conventional fuse boxes in favor of more modern and convenient circuit-breaker panels and designed a special internal radio

aerial system, with outlets in each unit which could receive the new television transmissions as well.

Although soundproofing was not an innovation—it harked back to the luxury apartments of the 1880s—it was unusual for the post-Depression era. Promotional material claimed that "each tenant will enjoy a quietude comparable to that of a country home," which the designer tried to accomplish by installing cork flooring, extra-thick concrete floor slabs, acoustic finishes on the living-room ceilings and sound baffles between apartments and around the public hallways.

Perhaps more of a breakthrough was the bounty of glass block, which Ackerman used instead of conventional glass windows. This cut down on street noise and brought large amounts of diffused light through the expansive openings without sacrificing privacy. It also disguised the lack of important views and reduced the solar heat load that the air-conditioning system would have to handle. Glass blocks were used to build an enclosed rooftop sun room (in place of a more usual penthouse apartment). In addition, the roof had a game parlor and a small children's play area.

After the building became a co-op in 1983, it underwent a longterm "improvement" program. In 1986, the original steel casement windows and the glass-block walls of the façade were removed. In their place came windows with thick, dark brown frames and dark bronze glass—a look more suitable to an office tower.

Unfortunately, 25 East 83rd Street was too far north to be protected by the East Side Historic District, and was studiously excluded when the lines were drawn in 1977 for the Metropolitan Museum Historic District. If the Landmarks Preservation Commission had been able to oversee the work, New York's first centrally air-conditioned apartment house might not have become just another badly remodeled building.

Figure 55. Period piece: as it appeared in 1938, 25 East 83rd Street offered the most technologically advanced comforts. *(Real Estate Record, courtesy of Christopher Gray.)*

Index

Ackerman, Frederick Lee, 77, 79
Aldhous, Frederick, 3, 4
Alimar Apartments, 8
American Institute of Architects, 20
Angell, Edward, 68
"Apartment Houses of the Metropolis," 7
Architectural Digest, 43
Architectural Record, 6
Arnold, Harriet Constable, 41
Arnold, Hicks, 41
Arnold, Richard, 41, 42
Arnold, Constable & Company, 41
Arthur, Chester A., 30
Astaire, Fred, 35
Astor, Vincent, 44, 63
Astor Model Market, 60, 63
Athens (Greece), 67
Avenue B, 44

Bagge, George A., 10
Bank of America, 39
Baptist Church of the Epiphany, 20
Baptist Home, 37
Bauhaus, viii
Benton, Thomas Hart, 53
Beresford Apartments, 67, 70, 74
Berlinger, Joseph M., 66
Birge, Charles E., 30
Blum, Edward, 13
Blum, George, 13
Blumenthal, George, 38
Bogart, Humphrey, 63
Bottomley, William Lawrence, 44
Brearley School, 49
Brennan, Michael, 68

Broadway, 6, 8, 10, 12, 60, 62, 63
Broadway Subway Line, 8
Brooklyn Museum, 24
Buckham, Charles W., 24

Camp, Frederick Theodore, 3
Campbell, Shiras, 60
Candela, Rosario, 44, 50
Cantor, Eddie, 71
Capitol Apartments, 13–16
Carlyle, Thomas, 6
Carpenter, James E. R., 39
Carpenter, John Alden, 53
Carrère & Hastings, 29
Casa Blanca, La, Apartments, 5
Caughey, A. Rollin, 53, 54
Caughey & Evans, 53
Central Park, v, vii, 16, 24, 26, 36, 71
Central Park Apartments (a.k.a. Navarro Flats), vi, 17, 53, 54
Central Park South, 24, 53
    No. 150, 53–56
    No. 222, 23–24
Central Park West, vii, 67, 69, 74
    No. 135, 49
Century Club, 17
Chapin School, 49
Charles, Prince of Wales, 40
Chelsea Hotel (originally Apartments), vi
Chicago, 51, 55
Chiswick, England, 60
Choragic Monument of Lysicrates (Athens, Greece), 67
Clarendon Apartments, 30–32

Clark, Edward, vii
Colony Club, 38
Commissioner's Map (1811), 36
Cook, Henry, 72, 73
Cornell, Katharine, 35
Cornwall Apartments, 10–12
Crane, Charles R., 39
Croff, Gilbert Bostwick, 3
Crowninshield, Frank, 35

Dakota Apartments, vii, 25
De Koven, Anna, 51
De Koven, Reginald, 51
Delano & Aldrich, 34, 35, 38
De Lima, E. A., 39
Delmonico family, 19
Department of Buildings, 20, 30, 34, 74
Deskey, Donald, 24
de Wolfe, Elsie, 35
Dorilton Apartments, 6–9
Draper, Dorothy, 54, 55
Dreyfous, Ludwig, 28

East End Avenue, 44, 48
    No. 120, 44, 45
East River, 44, 47, 50
East River Drive (a.k.a. Franklin D. Roosevelt Drive), 45, 46
East Side Historic District, 79
École des Beaux-Arts (Paris), 13
18th Street, East
    No. 142, vi, 3, 5
80th Street, East, 44
80th Street, West, 8
88th Street, East, 44

85th Street, East, 25
81st Street, East, 25, 44
81st Street, West, 34, 67
84th Street, East, 44, 46
82nd Street, East, 44
87th Street, East, 13
    No. 12, 13–16
87th Street, West, 72, 74
86th Street, East, 3, 4, 34
    No. 520, 44
    No. 530, 44
86th Street, West, 30, 72, 73, 74
83rd Street, East, 46
    No. 3, 41, 42, 43
    No. 25, 77–79
Elliman, Douglas, 29, 38
Elliman, Douglas E., & Co., 54
Excelsior Savings Bank, 66

Fairchild, John, 48
Farewell to Arms, A, 53
Ferguson, H. K., Company (Cleveland), 53
Fifth Avenue, viii, 3, 13, 17, 19, 25, 29, 36, 37, 41, 42, 49, 56, 57
    No. 998, 25–29
    No. 1020, 41–43
Fifth Avenue Apartment House, 25
Fifth Avenue Hospital (originally Hahnemann Hospital), 36–39
50th Street, East, 38
58th Street, 49
58th Street, West, 53
    No. 145, 53
55th Street, West, 49, 56, 57
59th Street, West, vi, 17, 53
    No. 150, 53
52nd Street, West
    No. 135, 56, 58
57th Street, West, 3
    No. 322, 59
Finkelstein, Jacopo, 56, 57
Fisk, Pliny, 17, 18
Fleischmann, Charles R., 25
Fleischmann's Vienna Model Bakery, 44
45th Street, East, 17
    No. 15, 17–19, 20
44th Street, West
    No. 27, 17
    No. 30, 17
43rd Street, West, 17
Franke, William B., 64, 66
Franzen, August, 24
French Flats, The (Stuyvesant Apartments), vi

Gainsborough, Thomas, 24
Gainsborough Studios, 23–24
Gerard, Sumner, 56
German Hospital (later Lenox Hill Hospital), 37
Gershwin, George, 35
Ghaleb, Dr. Gamil, 57
Gibbons, Grinling, 55
Gish, Dorothy, 63
Gish, Lillian, 63
Gordon, Tracy and Swartwout, 17, 20
Gotham Hotel, 56, 57
Gracie, Archibald, 44
Gracie Mansion, 44
Gracie Square, 44
    No. 1, 44, 45
    No. 10, 44–50
Grand Central Terminal, 41
Gray, Christopher, 53
Great Lawn (Central Park), v
Green, Andrew Haswell, 72
Grundy, Lester, 54
Guaranty Trust Company, 54
Guggenheim, Murray, 29

Hahnemann Hospital (later Fifth Avenue Hospital), 36–39
Hall, Arlington, 10
Hall, Harvey, 10
Hamilton Square, 36
Hammerstein, Mr. and Mrs. Arthur, 35
Hampshire House, 53–56
Hardenbergh, Henry Janeway, vii
Harper's Weekly, 51
Harriss, Dr. John A., 72
Harvard Club, 17
Hatt, René, 56
Havemeyer, Horace, III, 48
Healy, Thomas, 60
Hearst, William Randolph, 30–32
Heifetz, Jascha, 35
Hellgate railroad bridge, 47
Hemingway, Ernest, 53
Hesselgren, G. C., 7
Heuber stone works, 44
Hine, Lewis, v
Hoffman, Dustin, 71
Home Club, 17–19, 20
Hoover, Herbert, v
HRH Construction Corporation, 67
Hubert, Philip, 17
Hudson, Ethel De Koven, 52
Hudson River, 30, 34, 72, 74
Hunt, Richard Morris, vi

Imperial Apartments, 2–5
Institute for Deaf Mutes, 37
Ivy Club, 18

James, Arthur Curtis, 38, 39
Janes, Elisha Harris, 8
Janes & Leo, 8
Jefferson Memorial, 51
Jones family mansion, 44

Keaton, Diane, 71
Kehilath Jacob, Congregation, 66
Kennedy, John Drummond, 44
King, Beverly, 60
Kirkeby, Arnold S., 55
Knickerbocker Club, 38
Knole (Kent, England), 51
Konti, Isidore, 24
Kostelanetz, André, 48
Kranich, Victor, 22
Kress, Mr. and Mrs. Samuel H., 43

Landmarks Law, 36
Landmarks Preservation Commission, 6, 24, 29, 60, 71, 76, 79
Langham Apartments, 49
LeBrun, Napoleon, 3
Lee, James T., 25
Leland, Col. Francis L., 20, 22
Leland, Col. Francis L., development company, 22
Lenox Hill Hospital (originally German Hospital), 37
Leo, Richard Leopold, 8
Levi, Julian Clarence, 34
Lewis, Albert W., 44
Lexington Avenue, 30
Lignante, Eugene E., 53
Lunt, Mr. and Mrs. Alfred, 35
Lysicrates, Choragic Monument of, 67

Madison Avenue, 13, 20, 21, 22, 38
Manhattan Apartments (East 86th Street), 3, 4
Manhattan Apartments (West 52nd Street), 57, 58
Manilow, Barry, 71
Marbury, Elisabeth, 35
McDonald, Ronald H., 30, 32
McKim, Mead & White, 17, 25, 38
Metropolitan Museum Historic District, 79
Meurice Hotel, 53
Millay, Edna St. Vincent, 35
Mills, Harriet A. R., 20, 21, 22
Mills, Harriet A. R., residence, 20–22

Montana Apartments, 49
Moore, Mary Tyler, 71
Morton, Levi P., 29
Mowbray, William E., 20
Multiple Dwelling Law (1929), 67
Mutual Life Insurance Company, 32

Nast, Condé, 33–35
National Gallery of Art (Washington, D.C.), 24, 51
Navarro Flats (a.k.a. Central Park Apartments), vi, 17, 53, 54
Nesbits's Sons, John, brick and lime yard, 44
Neville, Thomas P., 10
Neville & Bagge, 10
New Century Apartments, 64–66
New School for Social Research, 53
New York Academy of Medicine, 17
New York Central Railroad, 41
New York County Bank, 20
New-York Daily Tribune, 6
New York Edison Company, 28
New York Journal, 51
New York Sun, 76
New York Times, 10, 39, 71
New York Title and Mortgage Company, 54
New York World, 51
New York World's Fair (1939), 74
90th Street, East, 44
90th Street, West, 10
    No. 255, 10–12
95th Street, West, 60, 63
94th Street, West, 60
Ninth Avenue, 3
Ninth Avenue Elevated Railway, vii, 5
Normandie, 74
Normandy Apartments, 72–76

Olmsted, Frederick Law, 72
106th Street, East, 37
112th Street, West
    No. 539, 13
O'Neill, Eugene, 53
Osborne Apartments (West 57th Street), vii, 25
Otis, Elisha Graves, 39

Park Avenue, vii, 3, 29, 34, 36, 37, 38, 39, 41, 51
    No. 280, 19
    No. 375, 49
    No. 470, 34
    No. 655, 36–40, 75
    No. 660, 39

No. 813, 57–59
No. 1025, 51–52
No. 1040, 33–35
Paterno, Michael, 41
Paterno Apartments, 49
Paterno family, 41
Patorno, Sullivan A. S., 77
Paul Weiss, Rifkind, Wharton & Garrison, 54
Pease & Elliman, 29
Pennington, Pleasants, 44
Phaeton Apartments, 13
Phipps, John S., 15
Phipps, John S., residence, 15
Pierre, Charles, 19
Pierre Hotel, 19
Pirrson, Hubert, & Company, vi
Pomander Walk, 60–63
Pons, Lily, 48
Pope, John Russell, 51
Pratt, Harold, 38, 39
Presbyterian Hospital, 37
Price, Bruce, 3
Prime, Nathaniel, residence, 44
Princeton University, 18
Pulitzer, Joseph, 30
Pyne, Percy, 38, 39

Radio City Music Hall, 24
Randall, Tony, 71
Ranger, Henry, 24
Real Estate Record and Guide, 13
Real Estate Record, 77
Rhodes, T. R., Company, 45
Rifkind, Simon F., 54
Riis, Jacob, v
Riverside Drive, 8, 72, 73, 75
    No. 137, 30–32
    No. 140, 72–76
    No. 440, 49
Riverside Park, 30, 72, 74
Robinson, Dwight P., & Company, 38, 39
Rockefeller Center, vi
Roosevelt, Franklin D., Drive (a.k.a. East River Drive), 45
Roosevelt Memorial Wing (American Museum of Natural History), 51
Root, Elihu, 29
Rose Associates, 59
Roth, Emery, 67, 70, 71, 72, 74, 76
Russell, Rosalind, 63
Russell, Walter, 24

St. Joseph's Orphan Asylum, 44
San Remo Apartments, 67–71, 74

San Remo Hotel, 67, 68, 70
San Simeon (California), 32
Schmidt, Mott B., 39
Schurz, Carl, Park, 44, 46, 48, 49
Schuyler, Montgomery, 6, 8
Schwab mansion, 72
Second Avenue, 3, 4
17th Street, East, 35
    No. 129, 3
Seventh Avenue, 17, 49, 53
Seventh Regiment Armory, 37
70th Street, East, 37
75th Street, West, 67
71st Street, East, 29
71st Street, West, 6, 8
    No. 171, 6–9
74th Street, West, 67
79th Street, East, 44
79th Street, West, 64, 65, 66
72nd Street, West, vii, 56
72nd Street, West, Station (Broadway Subway Line), 8
77th Street, East, 37
76th Street, East
    No. 55, 2–5
73rd Street, West, 72
Sheffield Apartments, 59
Shepard, Mrs. Elliott Finley, 29
Sherry, Louis, 19
Singer Sewing Machine Company, vii
Sixth Avenue, 53
68th Street, East, 36, 39
61st Street, East, 19
64th Street, East, 20, 22
    No. 32, 20–22
69th Street, East, 39
67th Street, East, 37, 39
67th Street, West, 24
    No. 27, 24
66th Street, East, 36, 37
Skyscrapers, 53
Sloane, William, 38
Soldiers' and Sailors' Monument, 74
Sotheby's, 53
Steichen, Edward, 35
Stokes, Isaac Newton Phelps, 39
Stokowski, Mr. and Mrs. Leopold, 48
Strange Interlude, 53
Strozzi Palace (Florence), 20
Stuyvesant, Rutherford, vi
Stuyvesant Apartments, vi, 3, 5
Sunken Gardens, 60
Sutton Place South
    No. 1, 50
    No. 2, 50

Swartwout, Egerton, 17
Symphony Space, 60

Taylor, J. H., Construction Company, 34
Thalia Theatre, 60
Thaw Harry K., 25
Third Avenue, 36
Tracy, Evarts, 17
28th Street, East, 30
21st Street, East
   No. 21, 3
23rd Street, West, vi

Vanderbilt, Commodore Cornelius, 29
Vanderbilt, Cornelius II, residence, 49

Vanderbilt, Gloria, 48
Vanderbilt, William K., Jr., 39
Vanity Fair, 34
Van Wart & Wein, 44
Verona Apartments, 20–22
Vienna, 10
Villard, Henry, 38
Vogue, 34

Wagner, Robert F., 54
Wallack's Theatre, 60
Ware, James Edward, vii
Warren, Whitney, 41
Warren & Wetmore, 41
Water Street, v
Weed, Hamilton M., 8
West End Avenue, 34, 56, 60, 64, 65

No. 265, 57
No. 401, 64–66
No. 925, 8
Wetmore, Charles Delevan, 41
Wheaton, Noah, family, 44
White, Stanford, 25, 35
Windemere Apartments, 3, 5
Wise, Frank, Building Materials Company, 44
Woollcott, Alexander, 48
Woolworth, Frank W., 43
Wyoming Apartments, 49

Yale Club, 17
Yale University, 17

Zimbalist, Mr. and Mrs. Efrem, 35